TODAY'S
ALL-STAR
MISSIONS CHURCHES

Also by Tom Telford

Missions in the 21st Century (with Lois Shaw)

TODAY'S
ALL-STAR
MISSIONS CHURCHES

STRATEGIES TO HELP YOUR CHURCH
GET INTO THE GAME

TOM TELFORD

WITH LOIS SHAW

Foreword by Leith Anderson

Baker Books

A Division of Baker Book House Co
Grand Rapids, Michigan 49516

© 2001 by Tom Telford

Published by Baker Books
a division of Baker Book House Company
P.O. Box 6287, Grand Rapids, MI 49516-6287

Printed in the United States of America

Library of Congress Cataloging-in-Publication Data

Telford, Tom, 1936–
    Today's all-star missions churches : strategies to help your church get into the game / Tom Telford with Lois Shaw ; foreword by Leith Anderson.
        p.   cm.
    Includes bibliographical references.
    ISBN 0-8010-6381-7 (paper)
    1. Protestant Churches—United States—Missions—Case studies.
    2. Missions, American—Case studies. I. Shaw, Lois. II. Title.
BV2410 .T45   2001
266—dc21   2001037488

For current information about all releases from Baker Book House, visit our web site:
http://www.bakerbooks.com

To Advancing Churches in Mission Commitment

ACMC has been a major factor in the U.S. missions movement over the past twenty-five years. ACMC's only agenda is to assist churches in finding and fulfilling their individual roles in God's global agenda. By synergistically linking missions-involved churches, ACMC has helped inspire and equip thousands of local church leaders to lead their churches to greater commitment and effectiveness in world evangelism.

To all the fourteen hundred volunteers, the coordinators, hundreds of speakers, and the U.S. Center for World Missions staff

You have made possible the Perspectives on the World Christian Movement course for the last twenty-five years. Your zeal and passion for God's glory among the nations is displayed by the fifty thousand alumni as they have touched the ends of the earth. Missions has been changed forever by your commitment.

CONTENTS

FOREWORD

Growing up in the northern New Jersey suburbs of New York City, I was an avid fan of the Brooklyn Dodgers. I collected all the Dodger baseball cards, waited anxiously for the newspaper to arrive each day with all the team standings, and watched every game possible on television.

In the fall of 1956 my father offered me one of the great surprises of my childhood. He had two tickets to the World Series between the Yankees and the Dodgers and invited me to take off school to attend the afternoon game at Yankee Stadium. My heart pounded with excitement as we climbed the steps to our second-deck seats along the first-base line. Since all my previous experiences with Major League Baseball were through black-and-white television, I was shocked to see how green was the grass. Everything seemed bigger than life—the smell of hot dogs, the hawking of the vendors, the shouting of fans from Brooklyn and the Bronx.

That wonderful day, October 8, 1956, turned to disappointment. Not one of my beloved Dodgers ever made it to first base. The Yankees not only won that fifth game of the series but went on to become the 1956 World Champions of Major League Baseball. Two years later the Dodgers franchise was moved to Los Angeles, and I never fully regained my childhood passion for the sport.

Years later I was a pastor in Colorado. One summer day I sat out on the lawn talking to a seminary student who was an avid baseball fan. He knew teams, players, dates, scores, and individual statistics. I told him about my first Major League game and the great disappointment that I experienced. He interrupted me with explosive enthusiasm: *"You were there? You were there when Don Larsen pitched the only perfect game in World Series history? You were there at one of the greatest moments in the history of baseball?"*

"Yes," I said, "I was there and my team lost."

Until that summer afternoon years later, I never realized how important an event I had witnessed. I honestly didn't know that a perfect game (when the pitcher faces only twenty-seven batters and none makes it to first base) is a rarity in any baseball season, but such a game has happened only once in a World Series game. I was part of history and missed the significance of the moment.

Some of the same emotions have run through my heart and head as I have read chapter after chapter of Tom Telford's descriptions of all-star missions churches. I am dazzled and delighted at the strength, commitment, variety, and effectiveness of churches across America that are fulfilling the Great Commission of Jesus Christ to make disciples of all nations. Some of the churches I know well, and many are new to me. Once again I realize that I am an eyewitness to the making of history.

Yes, there were great missionary movements in past centuries, but there is a great missionary movement in our twenty-first century as well. When future generations of Christians look back to see how and what God was doing to reach this generation with the gospel, I hope they read *Today's All-Star Missions Churches.* Even more important, may today's church leaders gather the payload of information and inspiration to build ten thousand more all-star missions churches.

Leith Anderson
Wooddale Church
Eden Prairie, Minnesota

THE ALL-CENTURY TEAM

More than fourteen thousand men have played Major League Baseball in the twentieth century. At the twilight of the century, a national panel of experts selected what they believed were the one hundred greatest baseball players of all time.

From that list of one hundred, two million fans voted and selected twenty-five players. Finally, a blue ribbon panel added five more legends to create Major League Baseball's All-Century Team.

With all the pomp and celebration of history-making events, on July 13, 1999, at Fenway Park in Boston, the All-Century Team was introduced, a gathering of the best talent the sport has ever known. The band played, the flags waved, and the fans roared and cried as the game's legends walked together out onto the diamond, and Fenway Park became a Field of Dreams.

In this, my second book, I want to once again set my passion for mission against the backdrop of my earlier career as a professional baseball umpire. While millions of Americans were spending 1999 selecting the All-Century Baseball Team, I was out crisscrossing the nation—talking, listening, researching, and polling church missiologists and church missions pastors to find out which churches are the top missions churches in America. It was the kind of year any baseball recruiter would wish for, a chance to meet the best of the best. Missions ministry is healthy, alive, creative, and innovative. I was encouraged by what God is doing in missions in America.

Not everyone agrees with the All-Century Baseball Team selection, and I am sure that not everyone will agree with my choices of top missions churches. But that's okay. This list is not a beauty pageant. These are not necessarily the biggest churches or those with the largest budgets. In most chapters I am highlighting a key church (or two) that does one thing well, a church that I believe has a place on my all-century team. I hope that you will find in these pages a model you can use, an example that might work in your church, or a dream you can share.

The churches in this book are "major league" because they are willing to let their game be watched, modeled, and criticized. They are open to share what they have learned—the thrill of their victories and the agony of their defeats.

So, let's play ball. Here's my line-up.

1

BIBLICAL FOUNDATIONS FOR MISSIONS

Bethlehem Baptist Church

720 13th Avenue South
Minneapolis, MN 55415
Senior Pastor: Dr. John Piper
Missions Pastor: Tom Steller

For most baseball enthusiasts in America, including myself, Lou Gehrig is the greatest first baseman that ever played the game. He was a true gentleman and sportsman, and, as his statistics show, he was unbeatable at his game. Lou Gehrig's career was cut short by a tragic, incurable disease. The last day he came to Yankee Stadium to say good-bye to his fans and friends, he stood faltering before the microphone and said for all the world to hear, "Today I consider myself the luckiest man on the face of the earth." The stadium erupted in thunderous, tearful applause.

Maybe I'm going to stretch it a bit here, but in Minneapolis there is a church that I am going to say possibly considers itself not the luckiest but rather the happiest church on the face of the earth. Bethlehem Baptist is a church filled with Christians who have a passion for missions. This passion is driven by a belief that missions must be the battle cry of every Christian and that God's glory and the enthusiastic worship of his Son are the goals of missions.

"Missions is not the ultimate goal of the church," says Tom Steller, Bethlehem's missions pastor.

That doesn't sound like the best way to get to first base in a book on America's top missions churches, but that's what Tom Steller and John Piper tell the congregation at Bethlehem Baptist on a regular basis.

"The glory of God is the ultimate goal of the church," they affirm. The ethos at Bethlehem is missions. Most people in the pew understand what missions means and where it fits into the life and breath of the church.

Piper says it best, "The final goal of all things is that God might be worshiped with white-hot affection by a redeemed company of countless numbers from every tribe and tongue and people and nation (Revelation 5:9 and 7:9). Missions exists because worship doesn't. When the kingdom finally comes in glory, missions will cease. Missions is penultimate; worship is ultimate. If we forget this and reverse the roles, the passion and the power for both diminish" (from *Driving Convictions behind World Missions at Bethlehem* by John Piper and John Steller). People at Bethlehem Baptist eat, sleep, and breathe this truth. It is at the heart and soul of the church. It's all about the supremacy of God in missions.

But it was not always so. Although Bethlehem Baptist had a great heritage of missionaries and missions focus when Piper came to be the pastor, missions was no longer a priority. Tom Steller shared with me a glimpse of Bethlehem's pilgrimage to their present place at "first base" in missions.

History

In 1890 Bethlehem Baptist Church, then called First Swedish Baptist Church, ordained and commissioned Ola and Minnie Hanson to work with the Kachin people in northern Burma. The Hansons represent the kind of early missionary that was sent out by the American Baptist Foreign Mission Board, before the Baptist General Conference had its own mission board. The Hansons lived among the Kachin for thirty-seven years, preaching, planting churches, and translating the Scriptures. In 1927 Ola presented the complete Bible in Kachin to the Kachin Baptist Convention. He returned to America and died shortly afterward. Since that time, there has been a people movement to Christ and about 90 percent of the six hundred thousand Kachin people profess Christ.

The esteem of the Kachin for Ola Hanson is profound and many consider him their spiritual father. In fact this esteem was so deep that in 1990 a Kachin believer, Hken Naw, made the pilgrimage all the way to Minneapolis to see their "mother church"—the church that sent Ola Hanson to tell them about Jesus. When Tom Steller saw this unusually dressed stranger after church one Sunday morning, he went over to introduce himself. Hken was studying at Trinity Evangelical Divinity School and told Tom how he and his wife, Tsin, had longed to come and see the home of the Hansons.

In 1995 Tom had the thrill of going to Burma to represent Bethlehem Baptist at the Kachin Baptist Convention. Instead of the three thousand believers that were expected, thirty thousand came—many to see the pastor from Ola Hanson's church.

Stats

Sunday attendance: 2,000

Missions budget as percent of total budget: 31 percent

Number of missionaries: 58 from home church (representing 235 people with children and spouses) 3 outside (representing 10 people with spouse and children)

Missions staff: 1

Most valuable missions agencies: Baptist General Conference
Wycliffe
SIM
Frontiers

The Kachin live in northern Burma—southern Burma was where the famous Adoniram Judson went to preach in 1812. The Kachin, however, were considered "wild dogs" and when the early missionaries asked the king of Burma if they could teach the Kachin to read, he laughed and pointed to his dog and said they would have more success teaching his dog!

When Tom Steller went to Burma, people came up to him, took his hand, and said, "Thank-you so much for sending Ola Hanson. We were wild men. Look at us now. God is faithful."

Tom says, "And now, the Kachin church is reaching out to evangelize unreached people groups around them in Southeast Asia. No glory to Ola Hanson. No glory to Bethlehem Baptist Church. No glory to the Kachin Baptist Convention. All glory to God alone."

In more recent history another event dramatically impacted missions at Bethlehem Baptist (BBC) in November 1983. The guest speaker for the annual missions conference was unable to come to Bethlehem. As a last minute resort, Pastor John Piper was asked to fill in. That event was possibly the single most significant factor in changing the face of missions at BBC. As John Piper prepared the missions messages, he was overwhelmed with "the supremacy of God in missions." He realized that missions is central to the work of the church and got excited about what God wanted to do. During the missions conference, his church caught the excitement. Preparing the missions message had presented a big challenge to John Piper, but God used it in the life of the church and in Dr. Piper's heart.

Tom Steller says that things in missions at Bethlehem Baptist have never been the same since. John Piper is a guy, who, like many other pastors, admits he managed to make it through seminary without taking even one course on missions. This confirms my conviction that if the pastor gets mobilized for missions, then the people will be as well.

One Sunday morning in March of 1984, Dr. Piper announced that anyone in the church who seriously and strongly believed that God was calling him or her into missions and would like to earnestly pray about it was welcome at the manse the following Friday evening. John Piper and his wife, Noel, calling it "Missions at the Manse," expected that thirty people might come. That Friday evening they counted about ninety people squeezed into their home. God was doing something.

This began a process of discussing what missions was really supposed to look like at Bethlehem Baptist. They asked, How does a church do a good job supporting missions?

Soon after that, another defining moment took place. During BBC's pursuit of an effective missions strategy, it was suggested that the U.S. Center for World Mission (USCWM), in Pasadena, California, might be a resource. Some people had heard about the Perspectives on the World Christian Movement course that was offered at the center. Perspectives is a course covering the biblical, historical, cultural, and strategic perspectives of world evangelism. This training program has had a profound effect on churches wherever it is taught. I can honestly say that in almost every church I visit, if the Perspectives course has been taught, or the missions staff has attended one, then they are moving and growing in missions.

About twenty-five eager Bethlehemites decided to take the course. They crammed into several cars and headed off to the U.S. Center for World Mission. Two weeks later they returned, informed and transformed. As they said, "We had our socks blown off!"

The outcome of the experience at USCWM was a bunch of mobilized members who wanted to make a difference in missions at Bethlehem. One urgent desire they had was to host a Perspectives course at Bethlehem. The next year that happened, with 120 people taking the course. They have offered it every other year since and Tom Steller believes it is one of the fundamental reasons the church sustains its vitality for missions.

Another crucial resource in the early years of Bethlehem's missions renewal was ACMC (Advancing Churches in Missions Commitment). It remains a vital source for Bethlehem's missions awareness, and regularly people from Bethlehem go to the national ACMC conference where they are updated on the latest strategies and initiatives in global missions, hearing creative ideas and finding out what other churches are doing.

Heart

As Bethlehem came under the influence of USCWM, ACMC, and other organizations, the leadership began to pray and work through what missions was supposed to be at BBC. Fourteen convictions came out of the discussions and study and are now the driving convictions behind world missions at Bethlehem. They are a powerful summary of the biblical mandate for world missions, the best biblical foundation for a missions vision that I have seen anywhere. As Piper and Steller say, "The leadership knows them and loves them and they shape all Bethlehem does." To be a part of the community of Bethlehem means to know these fourteen convictions. I will list them as they are described in the 1996 church publication written by John Piper and Tom Steller, *Driving Convictions behind World Missions at Bethlehem*. I ask that you read them through carefully, read them a number of times, and then read them and talk about them with the missions committee at your church.

Conviction 1. God's goal in creation and redemption is a missionary goal because our God is a missionary God. Jesus Christ himself in his self-emptying and in his identification with sinful humanity to the point of his substitutionary death on the cross is the perfect manifestation of the missionary heart of God.

Conviction 2. God is passionately committed to his fame. God's ultimate goal is that his name be known and praised by all the peoples of the earth. We believe that the central command of world missions is Isaiah 12:4: "Make known his deeds among the peoples, proclaim that his name is exalted."

Conviction 3. Worship is the fuel and the goal of missions. A God-centered theology must be a missionary theology. If you say that you love the glory of God, the test of your authenticity is whether you love the spread of that glory among all the peoples of the world. To worship him is to share that passion for his supremacy among the nations.

Conviction 4. God's passion to be known and praised by all the peoples of the earth is not selfish, but loving. God is the one being in the universe for whom self-exaltation is the ultimately loving act. The one and only reality in the universe that can fully and eternally satisfy the human heart is the glory of God—the beauty of all that God is for us in Jesus. Therefore, God would not be loving unless he upholds and displays and magnifies that glory for our everlasting enjoyment.

Conviction 5. God's purpose to be praised among all the nations cannot fail. It is an absolutely certain promise. It is going to happen. Nothing can stop him: "I will build my church and the gates of hell shall not prevail against it" (Matt. 16:18). "The gospel of the kingdom will be preached throughout the whole world, as a testimony to all nations; and then the end will come" (Matt. 24:14).

Conviction 6. Only in God will our souls be at rest. The one transcultural reality that unites every person of every culture is that God has set eternity in our hearts (Eccles. 3:11).

Conviction 7. Domestic ministries are the goal of frontier missions. What this means is that frontier missions is the exportation of the possibility and practice of domestic ministries in the name of Jesus to unreached people groups. The frontier people honor the domestic people by agreeing that their work is worth exporting. The domestic people honor the frontier people by insisting that what they export is worth doing here.

Conviction 8. The missionary task is focused on peoples, not just individual people, and is therefore finishable. Many of us used to have the vague notion that missions was simply winning as many individuals to Christ as possible in other places. But now we have come to see that the unique task of missions, as opposed to evangelism, is to plant the church among people groups where it does not exist. When the church has been planted in all the people groups of the earth, and the elect have been gathered in from all the "tongues and tribes and nations," then the great commission will be complete. The task of missions is planting the church among all the peoples, not necessarily winning all the people.

Conviction 9. The need of the hour is for thousands of new Paul-type missionaries—a fact which is sometimes obscured by the quantity of Timothy-type missionaries. Our prayer for Bethlehem is that we put a very high priority on raising up and sending frontier missionaries—Paul-type missionaries. Not that we diminish the sacrifice and preciousness of Timothy-type missionaries, but we realize what the utterly critical, uniquely missionary need is in the world, namely, there are thousands of people groups with no access to the saving knowledge of Jesus. Only Paul-type missionaries can reach them. That must be a huge priority for us. Without the gospel everything is in vain. A crucial role that the Timothy-type missionaries play is to raise up Paul-type missionaries among the peoples with whom they are working.

Conviction 10. It is the joyful duty and the awesome privilege of every local church to send out missionaries "in a manner worthy of God" (3 John 6). There is a big difference between a church that "has" missionaries (on the back of the bulletin or as a line item in their budget) and a church that "sends" missionaries. These missionaries should be grown and identified by the church.

Conviction 11. We are called to a wartime lifestyle for the sake of going and sending. To send in a manner worthy of God and to go for the sake of the Name, we must constantly fight the deception that we are living in peacetime where we think that the luxury of self-indulgence is the only power that can break the boredom. O may God open our eyes to what is at stake in the war raging between heaven and hell.

Conviction 12. Prayer is a wartime walkie-talkie and not a domestic intercom. In wartime, prayer takes on a different significance. Jesus said to his disciples, "You did not choose me but I chose you, and appointed you that you should go and bear fruit and that your fruit should remain *"in order that whatever you ask of the Father in my name, He may give to you"* (John 15:16). Notice the amazing logic of this verse. He gave them a mission in order that the Father would have prayers to answer. This means that prayer is for mission. It is designed to advance the kingdom.

Conviction 13. Our aim is not to persuade everyone to become a missionary, but to help everyone become a World Christian. Those who are not called to go out for the sake of the Name are called to stay for the sake of the Name.

Conviction 14. God is most glorified in us when we are most satisfied in him; and our satisfaction in him is greatest when it expands to embrace others—even when this involves suffering.

The conviction at Bethlehem Baptist is, "When it comes to world missions, there are only three kinds of Christians: zealous goers, zealous senders, and disobedient." It is their passion to "spread a passion for the supremacy of God in all things for the joy of all peoples."

My Call

What is happening at Bethlehem is not just a lot of talk and theology. It is total, biblically based involvement in missions. I am convinced that if churches in America were to get a grip on this kind of thinking concerning Bible-based missions, we would be overwhelmed and amazed at what God would do.

I would like to emphasize the comment in conviction 3 that "worship is the fuel and goal of missions." For some of us who grew up thinking missions was "on the bench," waiting to be called up for certain "plays," it is a paradigm shift to understand that worship is the fuel of missions. As people at BBC have studied Scripture, they have concluded that missions is not a program of the church. It is an act of worship. "To worship him is to share that passion for his supremacy among the nations" (conviction 3). I often tell young people that if they aren't called to stay in America, then they need to ask themselves where in the world they need to go to find more worshipers for God's glory.

Conviction 11 says, "We are called to a wartime lifestyle. . . . we must constantly fight the deception that we are living in peacetime. . . ." This is not the old simple lifestyle warmed over. This is the prayer that God would make us want to live out missions because we know that every moment there is a cosmic war going on between heaven and hell. Then we must ask what that means to our church and the way we live, worship, and do ministry. To grasp this conviction, I believe, will be to change the way the church does missions. An illustration in *Driving Convictions* helps us understand the wartime lifestyle. In World War II the luxury liner *Queen Mary* became a troop carrier. State rooms became bunk rooms with beds stacked seven high. All the crystal and linen were gone and resources were allocated to get the job of war done. How ludicrous it would have been, in a time of war, to see people lounging on the deck with mint julep and a good novel. War changes the way we look at all we have. As Piper and Steller say, "A wartime lifestyle presents itself not as a legalistic burden, but as a joyful acknowledgment that our resources aren't entrusted to us for our own private pleasure but for the greater pleasure of stewarding them for the advancement of the Kingdom of God."

Let me mention, finally, that Bethlehem has one of the strongest missions training programs I have ever seen. The heart for missions comes from the top down and from the bottom up and permeates the life of the church and the education and training in the church. Where missions is not preached from the pulpit and taught to the children, it is not found alive in the pew. Bethlehem Baptist confirms this conviction.

You may be anxious to call or e-mail Tom Steller or John Piper, but let me suggest that before you do that, read *Let the Nations Be Glad* by John Piper (Baker, 1993) and *Desiring God* by John Piper (Desiring God Ministries, Bethlehem Baptist Church, Minneapolis, 1986). Build your missions strategy and missions vision based on the glory of God and the supremacy of God in all things, and it will transform missions in your church.

Bethlehem Baptist's mission statement includes the concept of a biblical foundation that seeks to "spread a passion for the supremacy of God in all things for the joy of all peoples." This is certainly a great way to get to first base in missions.

2

EXCELLENCE IN MISSIONARY CARE

Hershey Evangelical Free Church

Hilltop Road, Box 648
Hershey, PA 17033
Senior Pastor: Dr. David Martin
Director of Global Ministries:
Betty Shaffer

I like Sparky Anderson. He was a baseball manager who spoke his mind and he's famous for his sayings. One was, "Don't embarrass me by trying to compare someone to Johnny Bench. Bench is the greatest catcher that ever lived." Hall of Fame biographers say that the Cincinnati Red's number 5 is the benchmark by which other catchers are measured.

In my opinion, Hershey Evangelical Free Church, and their Director of Global Ministries Betty Shaffer, is the benchmark by which other churches should evaluate their missionary care. If there's a way to make missionaries feel

loved and cared for, Hershey Free has thought of it. When
I say that, I don't mean they've just risen to the occasion
when missionaries need care. They have a strategy for missionary care that not only cares for missionaries when they
are overseas and when they are home but is designed to
help the whole church become part of that caregiving. The
result is a congregation that knows the missionaries and
feels a part of their ministry.

As Pastor David Martin says, "It's really all about people.
People excite people. People raise awareness. People express
compassion. It's through our people that Hershey Free can
care for our missionaries. But the fact is—this kind of caring must be fostered by a champion. Our missions council, led by Betty Shaffer, is that champion. I find that attrac-
tive. I would love to be a missionary with the kind of
support Betty and our missions people give."

As a growing benefit of the kind of care and attention
Hershey gives their missionaries, there is no letup in missions applicants from the church. Many people coming
from Hershey Free are Gen-Xers. These young people are
idealistic; they believe they can get the job done. When they
see the kind of excellent attention the church gives to their
people overseas, they are glad to be a part of the movement.
So what I'm seeing is that when you care for your people,
the benefits in mobilizing missions in the local church are
huge. I firmly believe that involvement breeds commitment. Hershey is evidence of just that.

History

The kind of care Hershey Evangelical Free Church gives
their missionaries does not just happen. In the twenty-
seven-year history of the church there has been a lot of
growth and maturing in the area of care. This evolution of
missionary care came from the conviction that it was the

church's mandate to step up to the occasion when missionaries were in need. To a large extent, the missions council has inventoried the congregation to find out what services and expertise are available. This inventory includes medical providers, financial counseling, housing resources, vehicle care and provision, places for retreats, hospitality providers, and much more. Then when a need arises, the missions council already has a resource list to draw from. The church is near the Hershey Medical Center, a nationally known medical complex. Many of the doctors

Stats

Sunday attendance: 3,200

Missions budget as percent of total budget: 28 percent (does not include short-term missions or large projects)

Number of missionary couples or families: 81

Missions staff: 2 full-time; part-time volunteers

Most valuable missions agencies: TEAM EFCM

and hospital personnel attend Hershey Free. The willingness of the professionals in the church to be available for important needs has made the difference in missionary care. The church has people ready to help, and the missions council stays in close communication with the missionaries, so they are able to be efficient and timely with care.

Betty Shaffer tells the story of church planter Tim McIntosh with Evangelical Free Church Mission (EFCM) in Peru to give an idea of how all of this works. Tim had a medical emergency involving a kidney. The missions council had been monitoring Tim's situation through phone and e-mail and knew that all was not well. Finally, the call came that Tim was in trouble. Because of a well-established network, the church was able to fly Tim to Hershey. Volunteers picked him up at the airport and took him to the ER at the medical center where Dr. Thomas Rohner was already waiting. This effort was successful because people were already in place for such an emergency. All Tim's needs for hospitality, recuperation time, travel connections, and medical attention were met. Recently Tim had a setback.

Through teleconferencing, Dr. Rohner, who has continued to keep in touch with Tim, was able to walk a doctor in Lima, Peru, through a medical procedure, and Tim didn't need to fly home.

Another missionary was brought home because of an emotional crisis. Hershey people had arranged for the missionary to be flown to a counseling facility in another state so there would be maximum confidentiality. It was soon discovered that there was a chemical need. The missionary was treated and is now back functioning well in ministry. This could have been a "burnout" fatality, but with close care, disaster was averted. Hershey Free believes lots of problems like this can be anticipated and corrected before they are full-blown, if attentive care is given right along.

I asked Betty Shaffer how this aggressive care works in relation to the mission agencies with whom they partner. Her response made me think of an excellent pitcher/catcher team. When they work together well, and understand each other's signals, you've got a winning combination.

Betty says, "When it comes to good church-agency relations, we'll find a way. I believe it is absolutely critical to have a good, open relationship with the agencies the church uses. This is a must.

"I go to every mission headquarters of the agencies from which our missionaries are sent. Yes, I do. I make an appointment to meet with the personnel officer. If that person changes, I go back and meet the new one. Once I've met them face-to-face and we've discussed our objectives and working relationship—then we can do the phone thing."

When I was a new missions pastor, I did the same thing. The value in that one face-to-face visit is worth every cent. I would encourage churches to make that a part of every mission pastor's or chairperson's job description.

Heart

The heart of the missionary care initiative at Hershey Free is not just to care for missionaries well but to develop knowledgeable caregivers within the body at Hershey Free. Missionary care can operate on a deeper level at Hershey because of networking within the church. This networking identifies people with resources and expertise to address a broad spectrum of needs that missionaries may have. As Betty Shaffer says, "We'll do whatever we have to do to facilitate meeting an important need of one of our missionaries. We consider that a high priority on the list of what we do here."

This is not just a great idea that Betty had; this is biblical. Philippians 4:10–19 and 1 Corinthians 8:1–15 confirm that genuine missionary care—tending to the servants of the Lord—is a mandate straight from the Word of God.

Help

Betty Shaffer and her team are brimming with new ideas all the time. Their list of creative services is endless. Here are some services that have changed missionaries' lives and even enabled them to stay on the field. At the same time they have changed the lives of people in the church. Missionaries have been cared for, and the church has learned how to care.

Communication. International phone calls and e-mail make the world a much smaller place than it used to be. If your missionaries do not have computers and the tools needed to be in touch often, you probably have some computer experts who could take some time to go and help a missionary get "set up." The missions office at Hershey Free often sends seventy e-mail messages in a day. It's not unusual for a missionary to get an e-mail asking what they plan to do for their anniversary that weekend, or when they last took a day off to relax.

Hospitality. If at all possible, provide housing for the home assignment of your missionaries. Having a comfortable place to come back to while traveling and ministering is such a blessing. Be sure to make it user-friendly so they can move in and out with just their suitcase. Arriving home after a twelve-hour flight, with kids in tow, is exhausting. Imagine a freshly made bed, towels hanging in the bathroom, and the necessities in the refrigerator. If possible, access to a food bank is helpful.

I remember a missionary telling me of a church that asked the families what their favorite junk food was and stocked the cupboards with all the things the family had missed when overseas in a remote area.

Prayer. Let missionaries know they are being prayed for. The single most important thing for the missionaries to know is that you, the local church, are praying for them. Send them copies of your weekly prayer sheet, the monthly prayer calendar, the missionary of the week, or whatever tools you use, to show them tangibly, that they are being prayed for. Expect regular prayer updates and needs from them. If all of your missionaries are on e-mail, you can let them know the day they are prayed for.

Every Monday morning a prayer team comes to the missions office of Hershey Evangelical Free Church to pray for the needs that have come in by e-mail, phone, or letter that week (sometimes as many as seventy in a day). This is work, but the team is well organized for effective intercession. The missionaries know this.

One other great group that prays monthly is MOMs—Mothers of Missionaries. Since many of Hershey's missionaries are homegrown, there are parents of the missionaries in the church. Who better to pray together than the moms of those missionary families? What a vibrant prayer group that is to visit!

Small groups. Missionaries need to have a small group who knows them, communicates with them, and ministers to them. Some churches call this group the missionaries' advocates.

There needs to be continuity in the leadership of this group so that the missionaries feel a sense of family when they return. If a class is assigned to a missionary, encourage the class to send a team to minister with the missionary for a week or so. Encourage the missionaries to communicate often with their small group, attend the classes or Bible studies when home, and be open with them about concerns and needs. People from this group could pick up the missionary at the airport, make a car available for his or her home assignment, and plan a refreshing getaway when he or she arrives home.

Short-term teams. Short-term teams who serve with a missionary become a natural care group for that missionary. Once the team has "been there" and "done that," they will develop a love for the missionary and the nationals and will want to pray, give, and stay informed.

Special field visits. Sometimes it is necessary to send a staff person, a missions council member, or an elder to visit the field and help understand or address a concern. This personal attention reinforces the importance of the relationship between the missionary and the church. The value of knowing that church leadership cares enough to take the time and make the investment to be with the missionary during a time of need is incalculable.

Pastor's visits. If there is one thing a church can do to let missionaries on the field know they are loved, it is to send their pastor to visit them. The added benefit is that the pastor returns with vision, compassion, and excitement. If you want to get the congregation excited about what God is doing cross-culturally, send the leaders for firsthand experience. What happens in the pulpit is reflected in the pew.

Accountability. "Failure to submit quarterly reports may result in the withholding of financial support." The missions council of Hershey Free is very serious about quarterly reports, so those words at the bottom of the report form are not taken lightly, but the missionary is encouraged to send in his or her short responses by e-mail. Over the years this short report has enabled the council and prayer partners to pick up problems and needs that require attention.

When missionaries complete and return quarterly reports, it helps them think through their goals for the next quarter and evaluate their ministry and family issues over the last quarter, as well as their personal walk with the Lord and their relationships. The missionaries understand that the requirement of this report is out of love for them and the desire of the church to see them fruitful in ministry. The result is openness and honesty, which enables the church to minister to them in meaningful ways. If the missions council doesn't hear from the missionary, the missionary hears from the missions council. It's as simple as that.

What does Hershey Free expect the missionary to talk about in the quarterly report? There are four categories:

1. Personal spiritual information: Discuss your devotional and personal prayer life; include details of how you are enriched, encouraged, discouraged, sustained.

2. Interpersonal and family information: Discuss ways that you interact and how time is planned for your family, close friends, and/or co-workers. Married missionaries should include information about spouse and children. Single missionaries should include information about roommates and co-workers. Please

include details of how you are encouraged or discouraged with these relationships.

3. Ministry information: Discuss details of how you are encouraged and discouraged about your ministry; include what goals have been met (or not met) during the past six months; discuss new goals and how you plan to accomplish them during the next six months.

4. Praise and prayer requests: Please provide details regarding answered prayer and praise, include ways that the missions council can address specific needs and ways that the church can be praying for you, your family, friends, and particularly your ministry.

Betty told me how two young single men from the church who were pioneer missionaries in a remote area felt that this reporting business was rather useless and took too much of their time. She told them this was a nonnegotiable and they would just have to do it as a responsibility to their church. Later on, on their home leave, she overheard them in a discussion with some other missionaries explaining how the reporting system, requiring accountability and goal setting, was probably the single most important thing in enabling them to succeed in that remote setting.

Retreats. Betty says that holding retreats for their missionaries provides opportunities for them to "tune up" spiritually. The missionaries prefer the Hershey Free pastors for speakers. The retreats allow time for the missionaries to be "family" to one another with time for rest and renewal, physical recreation, a special dinner, and often a special event like a day at an amusement park or a cruise.

Individualized care. Opportunities to receive sermon tapes, a particular new book not available on the field, graduation gifts for missionary children, baby gifts, cards and gifts for birthdays and anniversaries, gift certificates for dinner out when home on leave, a magazine subscription for a special interest, videos, CDs—all these make the missionary family feel loved and remembered.

Hershey Free's goal is to work with each one of the mission agencies with whom they partner. As Betty Shaffer says, "When the sending church, the agency, and the missionary are teamed together in partnership, it is a threefold cord that cannot be easily broken."

My Call

The missions council at Hershey Free is willing to share the ideas and resources they have. They have helped many other churches move ahead in missionary care. If you have a question, or need some advice, give Betty a call. Like Johnny Bench, "not much gets past her."

3

SECOND BASE

AFRICAN AMERICAN MISSIONS CHURCHES

Christian Stronghold Baptist Church

4701 Lancaster Avenue
Philadelphia, PA 19131
Senior Pastor:
  Dr. Willie Richardson
Missions Coordinator:
  Marva Washington

Buck O'Neil of the Negro Leagues used to say that you couldn't leave the game when Jackie Robinson was playing because he might do something you've never seen before. Buck adds, "He changed the way we thought about ourselves and the way we lived." Jackie didn't win— he triumphed.

There's a legendary baseball story about a Jewish family in New York City. It was Passover and the father asked the oldest son the ceremonial Passover question regarding the release of the Jews from Egypt. "Why is tonight like no other night?" The young man quickly answered, "Because tonight Jackie Robinson is playing in the Major Leagues."

I believe baseball changed forever because Jackie Robinson was not just a great player, he was a great man, and because Branch Rickey, the general manager who hired Jackie, was willing to do whatever it took to integrate baseball. These two men covenanted together to fight the odds, put their careers on the line, and make a difference.

I wish I could tell you the same story about the major North American mission agencies, but I can't. At the same time that Jackie Robinson was integrating baseball, missions agencies were afraid to push the envelope against racism. As a result, a huge potential missionary force was left unrecruited.

Since that was the case, African Americans who had a heart for missions were often unable to realize their dreams. This is all the more reason to praise God for churches like Christian Stronghold Baptist Church in Philadelphia, a church that moved beyond some of the mistakes of White missions agencies and leads the way in mobilizing African American churches for missions.

Stronghold, like Jackie Robinson, is not just a player; Stronghold is a movement. You can't leave the game at Stronghold or you'll miss something you never saw before.

Central to what is happening at Stronghold are Mrs. Marva Washington, the missions coordinator, and Pastor Willie Richardson. In my book, they are the Jackie Robinson–Branch Rickey team in African American missions today.

The purpose of the missions program at Stronghold, as Marva Washington explains, is to "mobilize Black churches to get the vision for world mission, to learn what to do once you have the vision, and to model the vision." Stronghold not only mobilizes its own people but has been used all over North America to teach, train, and mobilize other African American churches to respond to the Great Commission and "go." Marva laughs about a time she got a call from a Black pastor in New York City who wanted to come and see if it was really true that there were African American missionaries. He'd never seen one.

Marva admits that it was more than just the cold reception from White missions agencies that put the damper on African American missions. She says, "For a while we got sidetracked by the Civil Rights movement and that became our mission. Civil Rights became the first thing on the agenda for many of our churches. It was hard to separate the gospel from Civil Rights. It's hard to know whether the church would have been so involved in the Civil Rights movement if we had already been missions-minded and focused on the whole world." Marva says that's a question only the Lord can answer.

Stats

Sunday attendance: 4,500

Missions budget as percent of total budget: 10 percent plus a large investment in missionary care and training

Number of missionaries from home church: 12 families

Missions staff: 1

Most valuable missions agencies:
Carver Mission
Ambassadors Fellowship
Have Christ Will Travel
Cominad

History

So, how did Marva get to be a missions activist?

A few years ago Marva Washington was retiring from her many years as a teacher in the Philadelphia school system. She was also anticipating attending the missions conference at Christian Stronghold Baptist Church. She had just come from an ACMC (Advancing Churches in Missions Commitment) regional conference and was sure hundreds of people would flock to this church conference. Instead of hundreds, Marva found fifty people. Her immediate response was: "Something must be done." And Marva became the one to do it.

In thirty years, the senior pastor, Dr. Willie Richardson, had seen Christian Stronghold Baptist Church grow from a church plant with four couples, to more than two thou-

sand members and more than forty-five hundred in attendance on Sundays. From the beginning, Pastor Richardson
was missions minded. Missions was always on his heart—
but a busy pastor needs a team. One of his first commitments, as a new graduate of Philadelphia College of the
Bible, was to hire a missions pastor. So Don Canty became
one of the first, if not the first, African American full-time
missions pastors. Don Canty loved missions and went on
to become the president of the Carver Mission—an African
American mission agency in Atlanta, Georgia. His desire
was to have an agency that would gladly receive candidates
from African American churches.

Pastor Richardson was completely convinced of the
strategic role African Americans have to play in world evangelization. Marva's organizational and people skills along
with Dr. Richardson's vision and leadership became a winning combination.

Although they had found that mission agencies were not
receptive to their African American missionaries, Stronghold decided to constantly invite these agencies to send
their representatives to Stronghold's missions conferences.
At first they were happy if one or two came. Now they
often have close to fifty organizations and agencies come
to the conferences to display their materials and talk to
potential candidates. And over the years Stronghold has
found favor in the eyes of these agencies.

Marva recalls how a woman representative from a missions agency was very nervous about coming to inner-city
Philadelphia. She said anxiously, "But where will I park my
car?" And Marva said, "Right in the church parking lot
next to where I park mine every Sunday!"

Heart

The purpose of missions at Stronghold is far greater than
sending out missionaries from their own church. Marva

says she's becoming another missions mobilizer like me. I prefer to think of myself as the Anglo American version of Marva Washington. She gets calls from African American church missions committees from all over the country, asking her to come and help them with their missions mobilization. Stronghold has become a role model for other churches, even in areas of counseling and ministry team building.

"When I was a little girl, I always thought I was going to be a nun," Marva says. "When I came to Stronghold and heard about missions and met real missionaries, I was so excited about what God was doing. I met Tom at a missions conference, and Pastor Canty, and I had to get involved."

I had to ask Marva why she wasn't bitter when she considered how difficult it has been for African Americans to break into the major leagues of missions. "I don't have that in me because of God. I just don't have time to be bitter about the past. There is too much to be done, and the Great Commission is too important for us to spend any time worrying over the past."

Another hard reality African American churches had to face in the past was a lack of training because some evangelical Bible schools didn't accept any Black students. So even if there was a desire to be a missionary, often a young African American person never even got as far as the mission agencies, because he or she couldn't get training.

Marva says, "I may have some sorrow about this but I don't want to take on other people's problems. You see, when someone does you wrong, *that person* has the problem and why should I take on someone else's problems?"

Christian Stronghold's proactive stance reminds me of the Negro Leagues that emerged back in the early days of baseball. The excitement and enthusiasm for the game and the love of the sport birthed a dynamic league with players like Cool Papa Bell, Satchel Paige, and Josh Gibson. They used to say that Cool Papa Bell was so fast, he could turn out the light and be in bed before the room went dark.

The Negro Leagues filled a place in American culture that nothing else could fill. The same goes for African American missions agencies. Missiologists are saying today there are many developing countries that feel much more comfortable receiving African American missionaries than any others. This is a great window of opportunity for missions-mobilized African American churches. That's something we can get behind and pray about.

Help

Marva Washington is fond of saying, "That's an absolute must." So I asked her, what are the "absolute musts" in missions for the African American church? And here's what I learned:

It's a must that you share everything. The way things work in the city and in African American communities has traditionally been to share what you have. Christian Stronghold believes that you get more back when you give things away and there is strength in numbers. Whenever they have a missionary or a conference or a special missions speaker, they let everyone around them know. Within the city the emphasis is on cooperation not competition. Sadly, in the suburbs, there is often a one-upmanship attitude. An "our speaker is more well-known that your speaker" competition. Marva just doesn't see it that way. Whatever they learn or have, they share. At the last annual missions conference, seventy-five churches were represented and twenty of those churches were Hispanic.

It's a must that missionary candidates walk with the church watching them. "For three years you have to walk with us watching you before we will commission you to full-time missions overseas," explains Marva. Short-term experience is required before you can become a full-time missionary and all missions candidates have to be a part of their Way of Life evangelism team. They are trained to share their faith and their testimony during that time. "If they can't do evangelism when they are here at home," says Marva, "going overseas sure isn't going to make it happen!"

Candidates also take the courses Equipping for Mission and World Mission Today. They learn how to budget, write newsletters, and do deputation. Some of the intensive training was developed during the time when it was hard for their young people to get into evangelical Bible schools and colleges.

It's a must that you take care of your own. Christian Stronghold does not give full support to their missionaries. They take on about one-third of their own homegrown missionaries' support. They also help if they need a vehicle or special supplies, like a computer or a generator. The spirit at Stronghold is one that loves to be involved in their missionaries' projects, often sending containers filled with supplies to meet needs overseas.

It's a must that the church do missions education. Every Sunday, Stronghold takes time to update the congregation on what is happening worldwide. They have a weekly prayer newsletter and an annual missions conference. During the missions conference, they have a teen missions conference and a children's missions conference—so actually there are three conferences going on at the same time. The congregation receives a report once a month on current news from the missionaries.

It's a must that the church family show hospitality to missionaries. Marva told me with enthusiasm, "Our missionaries are loved. If they didn't say no once in a while, missionaries would be at someone's home every lunch and dinner for the whole time they are home."

Stronghold provides a vehicle and health care as needed to missionaries who are home on furlough. They have special care and support programs for single moms who go through the training and become missionaries.

It's an absolute must that the pastor be the key. The key to missions in the African American church is the pastor. If the pastor doesn't have the direction, the church isn't going to have any. Right away when you come to Stronghold, or become part of their staff, you know missions is prime. You know missions is going to get lots of attention.

Pastor Richardson says to the staff, "Even if nobody on staff gets paid this month, and there's no rent and no money for us—our missionaries are going to get paid this month." He says, "There is no way a missionary will ever have to come home because they need support. That's not even an option. If you're overseas, you stay there. When this church began, missions began. We've always had a missions conference and we've always had missionaries—from the jump start."

Dr. Richardson was head of the Board of the Carver Mission for some time, which shows you his heart for missions. He has the church send the whole mission board to Urbana every time it's held; he observes what the missions committee needs in the area of upgrading and sends them to conferences or workshops. He sent Marva to Liberia for a short-term mission before she could come on as missions director. He believes that his people need to experience missions firsthand. He travels overseas himself so that he is aware of what the missionaries are doing and what needs they have. Pastor Richardson says that Stronghold will never have a main speaker for a missions conference who is not a missionary. That is a nonnegotiable.

It's a must that missionaries report. Every missionary that is sent from the church must call Marva once a month, prior to the first-Sunday prayer times. They are to give a short report and a couple of prayer requests. Marva then presents these current needs to the congregation and they are prayed for personally each month. Marva says, "I'm not over there and the pastor will ask pointed questions about what they are doing and I'd better know the answer. I report to the church regularly on the status of the missionaries." Marva told me that there have been times when she has had to ask missionaries to come and get some help so they wouldn't go over the edge. She would never have known the urgency of their needs if they hadn't reported in regularly.

It's a must that all missionaries have access to the pastor and spend planned time with him when they are home. All missionaries must meet with the pastor personally and he spends time with them one on one. He takes the time to give them individual attention and gives them books to read. Recently he gave *Experiencing God* to each missionary. And he gives them other books and tapes, depending on what he hears. This personal attention is a hallmark of the African American community that I think could be a lesson to other churches. Missionaries are their ambassadors, so the church is committed to knowing them well and loving them very much.

It's a must that the missionaries are listened to. "I mother our missionary families when they are home," says Marva. "I observe their interpersonal skills because, to us, that is absolutely the bottom line. If you can't get along with people, you can't be a missionary. We work on that as they get ready to go. I don't want our missionaries to come home angry. Missionaries are real people and get upset, but I don't want to have them come home beaten up because they are angry and hurt. The church will send me to meet with a missionary where they are overseas if we realize there is a problem. I have been sent to the field to observe the dynamics of a situation so that we can intervene and help. It's also a must that at some point the missions pastor visit all our missionaries in their ministries on the field."

It's a must that missionaries be properly prepared in their personal life. All Stronghold missionaries have to take a course in biblical counseling before they go overseas. The first step in that course is counseling yourself. It is the desire of the church that their personnel go out with the tools they need to speak to themselves from God's Word. Stronghold cares enough to be tough. If missionaries are sinning in personal matters, the church will say, "Get it together or get home." They demonstrate a tough love.

It's a must that missionaries be sent out in teams. Stronghold believes in teams, and the church models teams in their leadership. It is expected that missionaries will follow that example. At the beginning of every year, Pastor Richardson has a retreat with all ministry leaders. He shares his heart for the year's ministry and hears from the ministry leaders about their plans. They pray and encourage one another and hold one another accountable. It's the same for missionaries. The church won't send people off by themselves. They try to have at least four people together. This helps in the area of accountability and helps the church focus on a particular area of the world where the team is. There is a team in Liberia, for example, and many from the congregation at Stronghold have gone to do short-term ministry with that team. They've sent medical teams, nurses, and medical supplies. Stronghold has about twelve medical doctors, several attorneys, and many educators in the church, so they have the resources to get involved where missionaries live and work.

My Call

Will the "Negro Leagues" and the "Major Leagues" of missions ever merge into one? I'm not sure that is necessary. African American churches, led by key, regional churches like Stronghold, are building on opportunities unique to their situation.

I am impressed with new initiatives that have been endorsed by many African American missions-minded churches. One such program is called COMINAD. COMINAD is committed to seeking out Christian Black leaders living here in America who were born in Africa. Many of these men and women came here for education or opportunity, fully planning to return to their country, but never have. COMINAD, which is located in Virginia Beach, Virginia, is dedicated to seeing how they can get behind any such person who would go back to serve in his or her own country in missions. It is simply a desire to seek out these people and make the opportunity available to some who, for whatever reason, have not returned to their country of birth.

The spirit of Jackie Robinson is alive and well in African American missions. I've been invited to speak at numerous missions conferences hosted by African American churches. The commitment to world evangelization is exciting and growing. Like going to a good baseball game, I always come away charged and glad I'm a fan.

4

CHILDREN'S MISSIONS

Mechanicsville Christian Center

8061 Sandy Grove Road
Mechanicsville, VA 23111
Senior Pastor: Paul Goodman
Associate Pastor: Pete Hohmann

When the votes were cast for the inaugural class of the Baseball Hall of Fame, Honus Wagner had the same number of votes as Babe Ruth. Wagner was fond of saying, "There ain't much to being a baseball player, if you're a baseball player."

Honus Wagner was brilliant at the bat, flawless in the field, and record setting as a runner. Yet his quiet humility seemed to leave him eclipsed by greats like the Babe. His eight batting titles are still unmatched in the National League. The great manager John McGraw thought Wagner was the greatest player—not just shortstop—of all time. The Honus Wagner baseball card is one of the most valuable in existence today. The card was recalled in 1909 because Wagner did not want it distributed with tobacco. Wagner, a non-smoker, thought it set a bad example for children. I think Honus Wagner would be glad to be identified with this chapter on children. He might say that there's not much to being a kid, if you're a kid.

I also think Pete Hohmann, missions pastor of Mechanicsville Christian Center, would further add that there's not much to getting kids involved in missions, if you get kids involved in missions.

History

The beginning of the phenomenal growth and success of children's missions education and ministry at Mechanicsville Christian Center began when Pete Hohmann heard Jan Bell, the founder of Kids Can Make a Difference, speak about kids and missions. Jan taught that there is no greater purpose we can impart to children than God's purpose, which is to make his name known to every tongue, tribe, and nation. Pete believes that kids don't have to wait until they grow up before they can understand God's purpose in our world. Kids naturally want to be involved.

You can't spend much time with Pete Hohmann without finding out that he believes that mobilizing kids for world missions is a proven method for mobilizing the whole church. It's the bubble-up effect. If children go to church and are told, "Sit still, don't make noise, and listen," that's exactly what they will do when they are grown up and presented with the challenges of world evangelization. But if they are mobilized as children, they will be mobilized as adults. And the thing is—I have seen Pete prove it at Mechanicsville Christian Center and I have seen it change the face of missions at many churches within his denomination and elsewhere.

Pete acknowledges the education he received from Jill Harris, the founder of International Children's Expo. He also appreciates other organizations, such as Destination 2000 and King's Kids International, that train children's workers in the church to mobilize kids. And Debby Sjogren, a member of Mechanicsville Christian Center, has developed excellent missions education materials for children.

Stats

Sunday attendance: 1,500
Missions budget as percent of total budget: 25 percent
Missions staff: 2.5
Most valuable missions agencies:
King's Kids International
Caleb Project
William Carey Library

Heart

Pete Hohmann's heart for kids in missions can be best pictured by a story he tells of a young girl at his church. When this girl was nine years old, she did a school project on Mongolia. One of the sources she used for her report was a Christian magazine called *Mountain Movers* magazine. The article she read explained how there were almost no believers in all of Mongolia and how many Mongolians place Buddhist altars in their felt-tent homes.

Reading about Mongolia and the altars profoundly affected the girl, and for two years she prayed earnestly and faithfully, night after night, that God would replace those Buddhist altars with Bibles.

Two years later, when she was eleven, this young girl saw the article "Hope for Mongolia" in another *Mountain Movers* magazine. The "Hope for Mongolia" article caught her breath as she read of a great revival and how five hundred people had come to know Jesus. She knew this was God's way of telling her he had answered her prayers. This young lady's name was Hope—Hope Smith. That day she learned of God's hope for Mongolia. The number of believers in that part of Mongolia has grown to more than two thousand and they have started a church. Its name? Pete loves to tell this part: Hope Assembly!

Many other experiences like this have convinced Pete Hohmann of the strategic importance of mobilizing children for world missions. For Pete, kids are not in little league; they are in the farm teams, ready to step up to the bat in the Major Leagues whenever needed.

Help

Pete makes no apologies for seeking out children's resources and expertise wherever he can find them. He is also generous in giving out whatever he has found. The day we met to talk about children's missions, I left with my car trunk filled with books, brochures, and manuals for doing children's missions.

I asked Pete to share his top ideas for mobilizing kids for missions and here they are:

Start a missions library for kids. This could be as simple as a Sunday school teacher purchasing some books and passing them among the students. At Mechanicsville they have a Radical Readers Room. This is a missions library for kids, complete with a huge wall map, bean bag chairs, and hundreds of books. This purposeful library grew out of an evaluation of what books were being checked out of the church library and who was checking them out. Eight out of ten books checked out were children's books on missions. The result was that this special library was set up for encouraging missions and an enlarged worldview. Some of the books are secular in that they are about cultures, nations, people groups, and geography. All the books are chosen to help kids think globally. It is one of the most popular places at church. I've been in there and it's a great place.

Use the missions P words. These words, developed by Jan Bell, help children think concretely and help them develop a missions vision and worldview. This is not a separate curriculum but a way of integrating missions into the whole life of the child and his or her experience at church. Here are those words:

Purpose: God's purpose is to make his name known in all the world. This is the point of the Bible. Genesis 12:1–3 tells us that God's purpose through the whole Bible is actually twofold: to bless us and to make us a blessing to all tongues, tribes, peoples, and nations.

Power: God makes his name known by demonstrating his power to people. As we pray, God's power is shown to people. Exodus 9:16 says that God shows his power so his name might be proclaimed throughout all the earth.

People: God wants all people to know him. People have been created with needs. We can help people know God when we meet these needs by being bridge builders between people and God. The name of the children's missions teams at Mechanicsville Christian Center is Bridge Builders.

People-moving: People are moving all over the world and this creates needs in their lives. At this point in history it is believed that half the world has moved to and live in large cities. God uses migration of people to make himself known to them.

Passport to the World: God has always told his people to go into all the world, but we need to know what the world looks like. We need to have a global perspective.

Preparation: Before we go into the world, we need preparation. There are many careers or jobs God can use to help others know him. God is preparing you now for his purpose and mission.

Possessions: Possessions are time, talent, money, and material things. We need to use our possessions for God's mission, not just for ourselves. We need to learn the difference between what we need and what we want.

Projects: We need to mobilize for action now. Sometimes this means giving our money for projects that meet the needs of people. Projects give us hands-on opportunities to make a difference right now.

Partnership: We are in partnership with God in the task of making his name known in all the earth. We can make a difference in God's missions when we join with other people. We all need each other to make God known to all peoples. No one group can do it alone.

Proclamation: Half the world still does not know about Jesus. We need to learn how to tell people the Good News.

Teachers use these P words as an overlay on every lesson they plan and teach. Can missions be seen in every lesson? Probably so.

Launch missions prayer for kids. Use "You Can Change the World" by Jill Johnson (O. M. Publications) in Sunday school. Start a special prayer meeting for kids that will focus on global intercession.

Start a monthly missions emphasis in Sunday school, children's church, or mid-week boys and girls program. Since many teachers are intimidated by missions education and will not initiate it on their own, Pastor Hohmann suggests a general session for all classes, with a "specialist" in charge. Invest in training your specialist by sending him or her to missions training events, such as the International Children's Expo or the National Children's Pastors' Conference.

Teach the kids the biblical basis of missions using the material developed by Debby Sjogren and Jill Harris, using the THUMB people. (See ordering information that follows.)

Develop a missions resource area for teachers. This may be no more than a designated cupboard. A central location for missions resources is essential so that they are easily accessible to teachers.

Provide opportunities for kids to give to missions. Kids respond to specific projects better than putting money into a big pot. Celebrate reaching giving goals.

Conduct a kids' missions retreat. Pete Hohmann says, "Our best retreat ever focused on global intercession. A group from the Global Children's Prayer Movement (Esther Network) led the retreat.

Hold a missions conference for kids during the regular missions convention. You could also hold it during a different time of the year so that you can utilize all your people resources that would otherwise be involved with the adult conference.

Encourage a Sunday school class to adopt a missionary, especially a family with children their own age.

Start kids' ministry clubs at church.

Start an outreach team composed of children. Contact Pete about Mechanicsville Christian Center's Bridge Builders.

Develop MED teams. Debby Sjogren has led the church in developing MED (Missions Education) teams, composed of adults who make a nine-month commitment to be trained to meet with one Sunday school class each month and in a general session once a month to disciple children in understanding God's desire that "all the nations will know him." Ongoing training and resources for adults who join the MED teams is provided.

Never stop looking for resources. Here are some excellent resources and organizations doing children's missions education. They are on Pete's "must have" list:

1. Unveiling Global Glory. UGG for Kids is directed by Jill Harris and is devoted to teaching the biblical basis of missions to kids. Jill has a video that presents this concept to kids through lessons, stories, activities, and games. Contact Jill Harris or Jennifer Ellis at jill.harris@juno.com or at Caleb Project, 10 West Dry Creek Circle, Littleton, CO 80120 (303-730-4170). You can also order the video online through Bob and Debby Sjogren at Unveiling Global Glory at www.jealous-GOD.org.

2. Esther Network. This ministry is devoted to mobilizing kids worldwide for the purpose of intercession. Several products that help teach global intercession are available. Contact Esther Network at 854 Conniston Road, West Palm Beach, FL 33405; 804-746-4303; lcci-eni@flinet.com.

3. The Great Commissionary Kids. Pete Hohmann is the author of *Mobilizing Kids for Outreach,* a book and training videos. It is a great resource for missions theology for kids, teaching about different mission fields, and equipping kids to minister to others. The *Mobilizing Kids for Outreach* book, tape, and videos can be ordered by calling 800-641-4310, order #715-LC–204. The cost is $20. Outside the United States call 417-862-2781, ext. 4009. Or e-mail The-Great-Commissionary-Kids@ag.org or mail to The Great Commissionary Kids, 1445 Boonville Ave., Springfield, MO 65802.

4. King's Kids International. Check out www.oufn.ch /kingskids/. There are at least nine area offices in the United States and Canada that you can contact for help and information.

According to Joyce Satter, a writer for King's Kids International:

Young people are looking for a challenge.
They want to know they can make a difference. They are looking for purpose. Although
Christian leaders have often overlooked
young people and made them feel unimpor-
tant, history shows that men like Adolf Hitler
did not. Hitler mobilized an army of children
and teens who were willing to die for his
purpose of world conquest. In a similar manner Communist leaders also realized the
importance of children and youth. After children were indoctrinated with the Communist
teaching, they were willing to lay down their
lives for a purpose greater than themselves.

From Pete Hohmann,
Mobilizing Kids for Outreach, 21

5. The William Carey Library. This organization's catalog includes many missions resources for kids at greatly
discounted prices. Write to William Carey Library,
P.O. Box 40129, Pasadena, CA 91114, or call 1–800–
MISSION or 818-798-0819 for a free catalog.

6. 21st Century Kids Connect. This web site—www
.21stcenturykidsconnect.org—has cutting edge arti-
cles, reviews of missions education materials for kids,
and a listing of children's missions education events.
The biggest event is the International Children's
Expo, which occurs in the spring of every even-num-
bered year and is for anyone interested in learning
how to give children a missions vision. It's kind of an
Urbana for Sunday school teachers, Christian school
teachers, home schoolers, children's church workers,
children's pastors, and Christian club workers. On the
odd years many areas of the nation have regional
expos, which are also listed on the site. Their brochure
states:

The vision of 21st Century Kids Connect is to respond to the critical need in children's ministry for equipping children everywhere to be full members of the body of Christ, fulfilling the Great Commission. In the spirit of collaboration and to enhance the children's missions education/mobilization movement, we have come together to: Facilitate communication and networking among individuals, churches, Christian schools and organizations. To promote research and development of quality and forward-thinking material. To identify resources and evaluate them according to Biblically, educationally and culturally relevant criteria, and to provide professional and lay training opportunities.

For information, contact Jill Harris at 770-631-9900 or e-mail jill.harris@juno.com.

7. The National Children's Pastors' Conference. If you are not a pastor, don't let the name of this conference discourage you. Actually most of the nearly four thousand attendees of this interdenominational conference are volunteer children's directors. For the past few years there has been an entire workshop track devoted to missions and outreach. Contact the International Network of Children's Ministry, P.O. Box 190, Castle Rock, CO 80104 or log on to www.incm.org.

8. *Kids for the World,* produced by Gerry Dueck, director of the Children's Missions Resource Center. This is the MOST COMPLETE book of MISSIONS RESOURCES FOR KIDS in the WHOLE WORLD. It's a resource book, not a catalog, but it gives information on where things

can be found. It is available through the William Carey Library for about $10 (see address under number 5).

My Call

Let me add here that Philip Renicks, the vice president of the Association of Christian Schools International (ACSI), says, "Challenging students to be world Christians must be at the heart of the curriculum in every Christian school." He believes that 21st Century Kids Connect is playing a significant role in raising up a generation of kids "who are obedient to the mandate of Jesus to take the gospel to the ends of the earth."

I get excited when I'm with Pete Hohmann, because he sees the future. Missions tomorrow will be the result of what is happening today in Sunday schools and the Christian education of our kids.

I remember speaking one afternoon to a large gathering of retired and senior missionaries. I asked them to tell us at what age they felt the call of God to become a missionary. The typical age was eight years old! Now, in baseball, managers spend a lot of time looking at the stats. The stats tell them who to play next and what the other team's strengths and weaknesses are. Without those stats, they would not know how to strategize for a win. If I were a manager and I saw that most missionaries are called into missions as young children, it would certainly affect my game plan. Wouldn't it yours?

5

DEVELOPING NATIONAL LEADERSHIP

Spanish River Church

2400 Yamato Road
Boca Raton, FL 33431
Senior Pastor: Dr. David Nicholas

I umpired for the Major Leagues in Philadelphia when Mike Schmidt played for the Philadelphia Phillies. He was a dedicated, hardworking player, and I agree with the many fans who say he was the best third baseman to ever play the game. You could watch him on the field and see his determination to win and hit and do his best. He led the National League in home runs a record eight times. Only Babe Ruth led his league more often. Schmidt and one other player are the only ones to ever hit homers on four consecutive bats in two different games.

Schmidt once confessed: "When I watch films of myself, I wish I'd had more fun playing. I wish I'd enjoyed myself more. But I was consumed with the pressure of trying to perform at a high level." Well, that self-imposed pressure may have taken away some of the fun, but it meant that he received the fourth highest percentage of votes of all time when he was inducted into the Baseball Hall of Fame. He was also inducted the first year his name was on the ballot. That honor has been given to only twenty-six players in history.

Mike Schmidt played his entire major league career in Philadelphia. He loved the team and was committed to doing his best for them. However, in 1978 after a difficult period in his career, Schmidt made a major tactical change at the plate. Schmidt was always a selective hitter, but in 1978 he started looking for pitches he could drive to any field instead of always looking for the home run on every pitch. "He changed his whole approach to hitting late in his career, which made him an even better hitter," said broadcaster Richie Ashburn. In 1979 Schmidt hit forty-five home runs.

About that same time, the Spanish River Church, a PCA (Presbyterian Church of America) church in Boca Raton, Florida, made a tactical change in how they played their missions game. It was a change that revolutionized their missions focus and changed their statistics forever as a missions-mobilized church. The model at Spanish River Church (SRC) is one that cannot be ignored in any assessment of missions churches in America.

History

I'll switch teams here for a minute and say that just as you could never get to first base in understanding the New York Yankees without coming face-to-face with George Steinbrenner, so you couldn't begin to understand missions at Spanish River Church until you've met Dr. David Nicholas, the founding pastor.

Dr. Nicholas founded Spanish River in 1967. It was a missions church with a nucleus of eight people who met in a small rented facility. Today there are more than two thousand members. But more significant than that, Spanish River has been used by God to help plant eighty-plus churches in North America and overseas. The number attending those daughter and granddaughter churches is in the thousands. David Nicholas is convinced that, for Spanish River, the way to do missions is to find dynamic, young national leaders, invest in them, and help them plant churches.

Stats

Sunday attendance: 2,000

Missions budget as percent of total budget: 10 percent plus faith promise

Number of missionaries from local church: Several but not with financial support

Missions staff: 1 (plus senior pastor's time and energy)

Most valuable missions agency: Acts 29 Network

In fact David was willing to let me quote him: "It would be just fine with me if Spanish River Church never sent another North American missionary overseas! In fact we'll probably never support another traditional missionary again." I asked David how he ever came to this point in his thinking about missions and, with the passion of a good umpire, he called it as he saw it. He described three defining moments in the history of missions in his own life and in the life of Spanish River Church that changed his vision about how to do missions.

Defining Moment 1: A Different Approach to Missions

David Nicholas began to review and evaluate the cost of sending Americans overseas to do missions work and came to the conclusion that it was very expensive and often not that productive. He realized that God has greatly used

American missionaries to reach many people, but now that there are Christians in other nations, it has become more productive to work through nationals whenever possible. Therefore, Spanish River made a decision to find catalytic leaders in other countries and work through them to plant churches, which become self-supporting in three to four years. This approach relies heavily on building personal relationships with people in other countries and not working through a bureaucratic system. Since their decision, SRC has planted forty churches, which have become self-supporting, in Mexico, Chile, Peru, Haiti, and India. A few of these churches have planted "granddaughter" churches.

Defining Moment 2: The Assessment Center

The next event that changed the perspective of recruiting and sending missionaries (which means church planters at Spanish River) was the development of an assessment center.

The denomination asked Spanish River to invest fifty thousand dollars in a church that was being planted in Illinois. Since they were convinced of the giftedness of the man who would plant the church, SRC made the investment. Pastor Nicholas says, "It all comes down to the leadership of the man. We are absolutely committed to the idea that if you invest in the right man, the church will be planted."

Pastor Nicholas believed in the importance of having the right man so much that he established the Assessment Center, a personnel clearinghouse for church planters for the PCA. Psychologists, counselors, and pastors spend three and a half days with seminary graduates and their wives and other leaders who want to be approved as church planters. They have psychological testing, aptitude testing, and several interviews and meetings. When the center is convinced that a man has the spiritual gifts and qualifications to plant a church, they seek out established churches that will financially invest in the church plant. The investment is enough to allow the young pastor the freedom to devote all his energies to ministry and not to worry about finances. This investment then diminishes in increments over the next three to five years until the church is self-supporting.

Defining Moment 3: Going International

The third defining moment came when the church realized they could take this commitment to investing in church planters internationally. Pastor Nicholas will tell you countless stories of situations where nothing much was happening in a certain ministry until a national leader was identified and supported, and then things began to move. The next challenge was how to identify, assess, and have accountability with church planters all over the world. A process of networking began.

Ernie Tomforde, who was the chairman of the missions committee during those years, knew that he needed to get plugged into a network that could provide guidance. He contacted me, since I was the regional director of ACMC (Advancing Churches in Missions Commitment) at that time. I put Ernie in touch with Woody Phillips, who was missions pastor at Church of the Saviour in Wayne, Pennsylvania. (He is now the president of United World Mission and Saturation Church Planting.) Woody made some networks happen. As Ernie said, "We weren't exactly sure what we were doing but we wanted to do whatever it took to increase missions vision in our church." It worked. The people at Spanish River began to get excited about church planting, and, even in the middle of an expansive building project for their own church, the people gave a surplus to the missions account.

The plan was to identify a qualified national pastor, using established networks, with the "gift mix" to be a church planter and then fund the new congregation on a one-time project basis. Support would continue on a descending scale over the next three to five years, at which time the church should be self-supporting.

Even the concept of the Assessment Center has been transferred overseas. The Presbyterian Church in Brazil has set up their own center, with funds provided by Spanish River. Six Brazilian couples have been assessed and five of them have been approved for church planting. The Brazilian church has made good use of the center. Before the center began, the failure rate for church planters was about 36 percent. Now that rate has dropped to just 5 percent.

Heart

A heart question at this point is how to get a church involved in a ministry that basically supports people who are *not* from the church. Here, in eight points, is the way it works:

1. A core value. Any person becoming a member of Spanish River Church learns this one core value: "The best way to communicate the gospel throughout the world is through strategic church planting." This strategy is printed in the orientation and welcome literature, evident when you spend any time on the church grounds, and clear as you talk to members.

2. Vision. The vision is part of the pulpit ministry. Pastor David Nicholas believes in this strategy with all of his heart. He preaches about church planting as a continuation of what Paul began in Acts. One readily available piece of literature at the church is his message "Acts 29: Churches Planting Churches."

3. Short-term. Short-term missions groups from the church go all over the world to assist their daughter churches in various projects. A daughter church may communicate a need for a new youth center in Mexico, for example, and, because there are already strong ties with this church, Spanish River can quickly send an enthusiastic team. They might send a team to India to do vacation Bible school or to Chile to train English teachers. The network is a well-established tool for informed short-term ministries. It is also a creative avenue for financial projects. Often people who do not give regular monthly support to a missionary get excited about giving to a big, unusual project, such as a plane, boat, or houseboat. The Spanish River VBS one year raised money for a car for a pastor in Peru. The possibilities are endless.

4. Network conferences. At least every other year, the Spanish River Church hosts a network conference and flies in all the pastors of the churches they have helped plant. The conference is for personal enrichment and renewal for the pastors, with sharing of ideas as well as some accountability. The theme of last year's conference was "Healthy Churches," and it focused on eight essential qualities of a healthy church.

All of the pastors are hosted by members of Spanish River Church. What a great way to get people involved on a heart level and make friends with pastors from overseas! The conference is an opportunity for pastors to nurture and assist one another, but it is also a chance for the congregation to care for them and learn how to pray for them. As a missions mobilizer, I see this as one of the most effective demonstrations of cross-cultural networking. It helps the people in the local church and it serves those from overseas.

These conferences have become celebrations of what God is doing through the commitment of Spanish River to planting churches. Oversees pastors see that they are in this together. They get away from their immediate surroundings and gain a new perspective on their work. Bill Ingram, a former missions chairman, likes to use the analogy of a salesperson's incentive trip. "Everyone likes to be rewarded for a job well done. After this conference, pastors go home more fired up than ever to carry on the work they've started."

5. *Seminary.* So committed is the Spanish River Church and their leadership to raising up church planters that they have begun a seminary specifically designed to train and transform those who believe God has called them to be church planters.

This fully accredited seminary has four outcome goals that describe the kind of person they are intent on developing. The goals, as stated in their 1999 catalog, are:

> To develop evangelizers motivated by Scripture and experienced in personal and group evangelism. To develop communicators who have a working knowledge of God's truth and are effective in communicating it in small and large group settings. To develop persons of character who are knowledgeable of the example of the Lord Jesus Christ and the basics of purity through the atonement of Christ; who are able to teach by word and deed and have a high quality of lifestyle and godly devotion. To develop leaders whose leadership is demonstrated by strong relations with followers, people whose lives are attuned, nurtured and enjoy mutual respect with the leader. They should be visionary, self-starters who are characterized by persistence, courage and creative strategic planning.

The mission statement says, "The Seminary at Boca Raton provides church-based ministry education that focuses on evangelism and communication skills and character and leadership development in lifelong learners for the planting and growth of dynamic churches."

Dr. Ted Ward, of Trinity Evangelical Divinity School in Illinois, and the Reformed Theological Seminary, through which the school is accredited, highly endorse the training model.

6. Acts 29 Network. With things moving well with the network of church-planting pastors, Pastor Nicholas felt led of God to start a new network of churches that wasn't directly part of the denomination. He decided to call it the Acts 29 Network and wrote up guidelines: The planted churches should be theologically Reformed, have a heart for church planting, and promise that when they become self-supporting, they will pay back the amount that was given to them to initially begin, and put 10 percent of their income into new church plants.

As he shared the idea with the church and others, almost right away, ten established churches responded enthusiastically and committed to the Acts 29 Network, agreeing to sponsor church plants.

A Network agreement was drawn up to show the relationship between Spanish River Church and the church plant. The agreement requires reports for financial and leadership accountability.

7. A grandparent's "brag book." You don't have to spend very long with Pastor David Nicholas, or any member of the missions committee, before he's pulled out the picture album and started talking about the "kids and grandkids": this daughter church that has grown to six hundred, and that daughter church that has just planted a church of their own. Or they talk about this great young church planter who got a part as Jesus in Jesus Christ Superstar so he could use that as a door-opener in the community. Or the Gen-X church in Washington that's bursting at the seams.

One of my favorites was the story of the church in Recife, Brazil, a city of two million.

In 1991 a great young man named Abner Assiss started a church in a carport in a wealthy section of the city. At first Abner wasn't even sure he wanted to plant a church, since he and his wife had started a very successful Christian School in Recife. But God moved in Abner's heart, and he has now planted six churches in Recife.

As Abner was planting his first church, a woman came to him and said she had a maid named Yolanda who often came to work crying because things were so terrible at home. Yolanda's husband drank his pay away and there was no food on the table, no food for the kids. So the woman asked Abner if he would talk to Yolanda and her husband, Fernando. Abner talked to them and invited them to church. This couple lived in a very poor area but attended the church and soon came to know the Lord and were wonderfully saved.

Yolanda and Fernando asked Abner if he would come and start a church in their neighborhood. Abner didn't even have a building for the first church, which was growing. But, in spite of that, this young church bought a house in Yolanda and Fernando's neighborhood and started a church there. Since that time, Spanish River Church has purchased another house in that area where Abner has started a clinic to provide medical services for the people in the neighborhood. As of this date, Abner has planted six churches and has an institute to train people to plant other churches. Now that's something the people at Spanish River really get excited about!

8. *Finances.* "We run lean here," says Pastor David Nicholas. "We have only two committees, the missions committee and the school board. And both of these report to the elders. So we can make decisions pretty quickly and it has worked very well for the church. We have seven elders. The church tithes 10 percent of its budget to missions,

but usually, because of special projects, we give much more than that."

My Call

If a person comes to the missions chairman at Spanish River Church and says that their grandson is going with XYZ mission and would like to meet with him to present his ministry and needs, they would get a polite no. Not because the ministry isn't good and not because the mission isn't good—but that is *not* what Spanish River is all about. Traditional missions should be carried on, says the missions committee, but not by Spanish River.

For a church trying to play the game well, I'd say the people of Spanish River have their bases covered and have hit some creative home runs. It's not for everybody, but for Spanish River it's the right call.

6

RETHINKING MISSION PARADIGMS

Park Street Church

1 Park Street
Boston, MA 02108
Senior Pastor:
  Dr. Gordon Hugenberger
Minister of Missions:
  Casely B. Essamuah

You could almost run from Fenway Park to Park Street Church in Boston during the seventh inning stretch. For many Bostonians, both structures are places of worship.

One of the greatest ball players to ever swing a bat for the Red Sox in Fenway Park was Ted Williams. They used to say that trying to get the ball past Ted Williams was like trying to get a sunbeam past a rooster—it just can't be done. When Ted Williams was a rookie, he used to say, "All I want in life is that someday when I walk down the street, people will look at me and say, 'There goes the greatest baseball hitter that ever lived.'"

73

There was a time in Ted Williams's life when he made a career-defining decision. As the 1941 season was ending, Ted was holding a .400 average. If he sat out the last two games of the season, that average would not be compromised. He would stay "the greatest." However, if he played the last two games and didn't hit very well, his average could go down. Against the recommendation of many friends and counselors, he played the last two games—and his average went up with six hits out of eight at bats!

Back across the city, Park Street Church, which will turn two hundred years old this decade, made a huge church-defining decision that had the potential to make or break its historical position as a strong, missions-mobilized church.

History

Let's put Park Street Church into historical perspective. It has been a pacesetting church in missions since its founding in 1809, a major player in the history of missions in North America. It helped establish the American Board of Commissioners for Foreign Service, and among its first missionaries were Adoniram Judson and Samuel J. Mills. In this century, Dr. Harold J. Ockenga, after spending time with Dr. Oswald J. Smith of Peoples Church in Toronto, Canada, initiated the church's large missions conferences. In 1940, as these conferences with their emphasis on faith promise began, the missions giving of Park Street Church increased in huge increments. In those days missionaries were often sent out fully supported by the church. At one time there were well over one hundred missionaries.

Park Street was known all over the nation as a missions church and an evangelistic church. The famous corner in Boston, where Park Street sits with an outdoor balcony for preaching, was the scene of many huge crusades. Students from Boston's fifty or more colleges and universities came to Park Street and it was there that many felt the call to full-time missions. Two hundred years of missions—what a legacy! Casely Essamuah estimates that Park Street has sent out more than three hundred full-time missionaries and given over thirty million dollars to missions in the last sixty years.

Casely Essamuah, the present minister of missions, is Ghanaian-born and a Harvard graduate—one of the many students who came to Park Street during their university careers. As a student he became involved in the ministry of the church and now is on staff. He has been a point man for this major church-defining transition that Park Street began in 1997.

Stats

Sunday attendance: 2,000

Missions giving: Over 1.25 million dollars last year

Number of missionaries: 14 at full support, others being phased or transferring

Missions staff: 1 full-time minister, 1 full-time employee, 2 part-time employees, 1 seminary intern, missionaries on furlough

Most valuable missions agencies: agencies of supported missionaries

When this new idea was introduced to the church at large, it was the beginning of a very difficult time. Casely admitted that he even got hate letters from some of the members and comments like, "You've all gone nuts!" However, the strong commitment of the senior pastor and elders at the church to the new model kept things moving toward their new vision.

So what was this change and how did it happen?

Heart

On December 5, 1997, Dr. Gordon Hugenberger, the senior minister at Park Street Church, sent a letter to each missionary supported by the church. The letter was written on behalf of the Missions Committee. It contained answers to many important questions that had come up during the intense dialogue at the church as this decision was in process. With permission from Casely Essamuah, what follows are excerpts from that letter, which will help you understand the heart of the matter.

> Dear Missionary of Park Street Church:
>
> On November 4 the Missions Committee of Park Street Church voted unanimously to adopt a new policy that is intended to radically strengthen the relationship between our church and our active missionaries. Within a mutually agreeable time frame, we will work to redefine our relationship with our active missionaries so that they will be considered as *members of our church's ministerial staff,* except that they will be seconded to various missionary organizations, other than during furloughs.
>
> This change obviously signals a paradigm shift in how we conceive of our relationship to our missionaries. . . .
>
> In view of this, our policy will be to provide *full financial support* . . . just as we would for any other member of our ministerial staff. In turn, as with any other member of our staff it will be expected that our missionaries will consider Park Street Church to be their home church. . . . Further, without diminishing the indispensable role of missions agencies, it is expected that our missionaries would seek to involve Park Street Church in any and all major decisions that affect their ministries. Finally, when they are not away on the field, missionaries should normally spend their furloughs at Park Street Church. Although missionaries would be free for outside speaking engagements as required by their missions agencies, furloughs should be designed mainly for rest, time with family, further study, writing and significant fellowship and ministry at Park Street Church in keeping with the missionary's gifts.
>
> What has prompted this change in policy?
>
> Older missionaries [of Park Street] will recognize that this "new" policy is largely a return to the practice of Park Street Church at the height of its missions program. . . . At

that time Park Street Church typically provided full financial support to the missionaries it sent out. Later, increased administrative costs for missions agencies, inflation and diminished missions giving at Park Street forced an adjustment in the original policy. Rather than reduce the number of missionaries being supported, it was decided to reduce the amount of support to be offered to each missionary. This erosion of support continued. Support now is on average 15% of what missionaries require. Consequently most missionaries have to maintain relationships with a large number of supporting churches, which are often spread out over a vast geographical area. Missiologists have long lamented the obvious inefficiency, impracticality and inadequacy of such a system of support.

An acute manifestation of these difficulties is seen in the contemporary practice of the "furlough." Rather than refreshing and strengthening the missionary and providing needed opportunities for further training, furloughs or "home ministry assignments," all too often feel like a rat race. In an attempt to shore up tenuous support from a large array of churches, the missionary has to contend with the stress of constant travel, meetings, and speaking engagements, often away from his or her family. Not surprisingly, many excellent missionaries have been diverted from the field by the understandable attraction of salaried ministries that don't require this kind of exhausting deputation.

The results of the modern furlough are no less frustrating for the supporting churches. Although the pastor or a host family may have the privilege of less formal conversation and prayer with the missionary, contact with the church as a whole is generally restricted to a cameo appearance at a Sunday service, one or two presentations and a covered dish supper. Consequently the church fails to move beyond a superficial knowledge of its missionaries or their needs and joys. *This would be fine if we did not believe in prayer.* . . . Jesus declared, "Where your treasure is, there your heart will be also" (Matthew 6:21). We seem to be intent on defying this principle when we expect churches to have their hearts with a missionary in whose ministry they are investing at such a meager level.

Dr. Hugenberger went on in the letter to raise questions about finances. He also addressed the question of the timing of the changes and finances and the possibility that missionaries would say no to the proposal.

By 1999 the proposal was fully implemented and eight missionaries began to be fully supported by Park Street Church. The church went from around thirty-five missionaries at 35 percent support to eight at 100 percent! By the end of 2000 there were fourteen missionaries at 100 percent support with seventeen active missionaries and thirty-four retired missionaries still receiving partial support.

Before this new 100 percent support venture began, missions giving at Park Street had been in decline over a number of years. However, since the new program has begun, giving has increased and in 1999 the missions budget ended with a surplus. The belief of the leadership was that giving would increase when there was a significant investment in fewer missionaries. As far as Park Street goes—they were right. The year 1999 saw the decrease in giving ending and the goal of 1.25 million dollars exceeded.

This new model meant that missionaries needed to contact all their other supporting churches to tell them that their support was no longer needed. As the letter explained, "It is hoped that your other churches will use those funds to increase the level of their support for their other missionaries, or they will use them to send out other missionaries."

Although this was a phenomenal shift, Casely Essamuah says that three things kept the church on target and involved during this change: "The commitment from the leadership and the pulpit, the outstanding expository preaching and dealing with the issue from a biblical perspective, and the strong historical base in foreign missions. Park Street has always had an identity as a missions-mobilized church. There was a sense from the body that this could not be lost.

In case you should get the impression that Park Street Church is all about supporting fourteen missionaries at full support, let me tell you that you would be very mistaken. Those fourteen missionaries are only one part of an extensive missions outreach and vision. Here are some highlights of the Park Street missions program:

A comprehensive 10-day missions conference. Park Street is one of the few churches that still maintains the traditional weeklong conference. This one even goes to ten days. It includes classes of the fourteen-week Perspectives course offered by the U.S. Center for World Mission, a full-blown children's conference, seminars on subjects like "The Unfamiliar Passions of God: Justice and Global Witness," prayer breakfasts, tentmaking workshops, and reports from the missionaries who all attend the conference.

Barnabas teams. A Barnabas team is a group of eight to twelve who take the responsibility for supporting a missionary by making sure that missionary is integrated into the life and care of the church as fully as possible. The team is the primary link between the missionary and the church. Each member of the team makes a commitment to three things: prayer, communication with the missionary, and meeting together with the whole Barnabas team at least once every two months. These teams receive the missionaries when they are home and make sure their physical and spiritual needs are met. At present a seminary student who is interning at Park Street Church coordinates these teams. There is extensive training and guidance for these Barnabas teams.

International ministry partners. Park Street Church partners with international leaders from ministries overseas. For example, they invest in the Croatia Evangelical Theological Seminary, Prague Evangelical Theological Seminary, and the South Asia International Fellowship of Evangelical Students.

Short-term missions trips. At any time during the year, there are short-term missions trips in progress. Many of these are organized through mission agencies as well as directly with full-time missionaries that Park Street supports.

Ministry to internationals. Because Park Street Church is strategically located at the hub of the American city with the most college students per capita, they have the unique opportunity to reach out to international students from all over the world. Casely believes that this is one of the strongest ministries of the church. All day, and almost all night, the doors of the church are open to students for counseling, conversation, friendship, and the gospel. Historically, a ministry to international students has been a hallmark of the church. Recently this ministry has seen growth and focus.

City works. Each member of Park Street is encouraged to get involved in a ministry in the city of Boston. Lots of information for involvement as well as a hotline are available to keep members aware of current ministry needs in the city.

Help

Dr. Gordon Hugenberger and Pastor Casely Essamuah have done biblical research and developed quite a lot of material on the "full-support paradigm for missions support." They have had to expound and defend it well, especially to the congregation in the early stages. They refer to OMF (Overseas Missionary Fellowship) missiologist, Michael Griffith, who advocates this strategy in his book *Get Your Church Involved in Missions* (OMF, 1972). I have no question that this is a workable paradigm for some churches. What is amazing is that a large historic church like Park Street Church could make the shift at this time in their history.

Although I have focused on many of the positive effects of adopting a full-support policy, Casely reminds me that it is also important to note the struggles that they have had to face. Because it is important to understand this from as many angles as possible, here are three significant struggles for any church contemplating a full-support policy.

1. Missionaries, who have to choose between supporting churches, may suffer emotional turmoil. If they begin to receive full support from Park Street Church, it means ending support relationships with other churches with whom strong bonds may have developed. This would be a difficult decision for most missionaries.

2. Sister churches may not understand the new concept and may resent your taking "their" missionaries. There is either a feeling of being "bought out" by a church offering full support or, if a missionary declines full support, then other churches have to struggle to make up the difference.

3. There is the prospect of taking on more missionaries than you can afford. Currently Park Street has fourteen missionaries at full support, and by the end of the year 2000, they were operating at a deficit. Full support for missionaries will mean putting a cap on the number of missionaries a church can support.

Park Street Pastor Gordon Hugenberger wants to emphasize this very important fact: "We are not choosing the full-support policy to guarantee success. Much of what we are attempting to do, we are doing not merely because we think it will be more successful—the fact is it may or may not be—but because we honestly believe it better reflects the priorities and approach of the New Testament church. If it didn't, we wouldn't be interested."

My Call

Let me respond to a couple of comments in the church letter. I would have to agree with Dr. Hugenberger that the average person in the pew in many churches doesn't know the missionaries well enough to really pray. In fact when quizzes are given at missions conferences, I've often seen that church members are hard put to name all the missionaries, much less their children, or what ministries the missionaries are involved in. If the church sees a missionary only for a "cameo" moment on Sunday every four years and the turnover in many churches is around 50 percent every three years—then we do have a problem with effective praying. Having fewer missionaries who are more visible, more often sounds like one good solution.

It's hard to argue with the increase in giving and involvement of the church. The Barnabas teams—with around ten members on each team—translate to 140 people for this church with 14 missionaries. Having 140 missions activists in the church already is a shot in the arm for missions.

I am also encouraged that Park Street is aggressively seeking partnerships with international leaders and ministries. The commitment to these partnerships will keep the scope of world evangelization broad enough, even though the missionaries they support may be fewer.

With committed leadership who believe this is a biblical mandate, this will work. Dr. Hugenberger likes to quote Dr. John Haggai who said, "Attempt something so great for God that it's doomed to failure unless God be in it." Dr.

Hugenberger adds, "We want to be that kind of a church, a church whose vitality and love for each other cannot be explained apart from God."

This is the kind of team a good scout likes to keep his eye on.

7

DENOMINATIONAL MISSIONS AGENCIES
Total Church Involvement

Fairhaven Church

637 E. Whipp Road
Dayton, OH 45459
Senior Pastor: Pete Schwalm
Associate Pastor for International
Ministries: David Smith

Some say that Babe Ruth was not only the most famous baseball player of all time, he was the most famous player in any sport in the twentieth century. During his time, he hit more home runs than the rest of the league put together. It's hard for us today to imagine the impact of the man on America. Sportswriter Tommy Holmes said, "Twenty years ago I stopped writing about the Babe for the simple reason that I realized that those who had never seen him didn't believe me."

One comment that the "Sultan of Swat" made that puts him on my list of greats was this: "The way a team plays as

a whole determines its success. You may have the greatest
bunch of individual stars in the world, but if they don't play
together, the club won't be worth a dime."

Pastor Pete Schwalm of Fairhaven Church implements that
same commitment in the way he leads the community at his
church. He is committed to the idea that the church is not a
team with a few leadership "stars" but a whole community
in which each player has a particular role, understands that
role, and participates fully in the ministry of the church.

History

In 1983 Fairhaven Church, a Christian and Missionary
Alliance Church, called Rev. Forrest (Pete) Schwalm to be
their pastor. Traditionally all missionaries and monies for
missions, as well as all recruitment and sending of CMA
missionaries, was done through a central missions department of the Christian and Missionary Alliance. The church
had a dilemma. They wanted to be supportive of denominational missions but they wanted the excitement of sending their own missionaries and of faith promise giving.

Here's some background about Fairhaven's solution to
their dilemma. This is an excerpt from *Mobilizer* (vol. 9, no.
2, p. 13):

> Pete Schwalm . . . and the church leaders felt that the
> church had a biblical obligation to the missionary candi-
> dates that had been mobilized by the church. But this was
> an Alliance church committed to the Alliance Faith Promise
> program, which at that time was required of all churches in
> the denomination. The solution they devised has the bless-
> ing of the CMA denomination and might serve as a model
> for other denominational churches. . . . They drew up a
> sophisticated evaluation system to be applied to non-
> Alliance missionaries. This model assigns weights to vari-

ous types of missions such as the growth and development of the national church and evangelizing hidden/unreached peoples. By means of this mechanism they make their decisions regarding the support of individual missionaries.

At the same time, the church leaders formulated long-range goals for increasing the percentage of church income to be distributed outside the church itself.

They established an inclining scale, intending by 2005 to be sending 40 percent of their operating funds to missions, both local and cross cultural. . . . This would still keep them in the higher ranks of churches that support the CMA Great Commissions fund, while at the same time enabling them to exercise good stewardship with regard to other missionaries, based on their stated values. . . . No wonder the denomination has granted written permission for this church to pursue this broad vision!

Stats

Sunday attendance: 2,000

Missions budget as percent of total budget: nearing goal of 30 percent

Number of missionaries supported: 64

Missions staff: 2

Most valuable missions agency: Christian Missionary Alliance (CMA)

I have known Pete Schwalm for a number of years because he has served on the board of ACMC (Advancing Churches in Missions Commitment). As I have observed Pete, I have seen two things that are hallmarks of his leadership. First, Pete is committed to investing in his leadership team in extraordinary ways. Second, Pete is dedicated to making sure that every member of the church is on an intentionally designed track to move them through four stages of church involvement. The fourth and culminating stage is a covenant to participate in the global cause of Christ. This will be discussed later in the chapter.

The leadership of the Fairhaven Church felt that this deliberate model—participating in the global cause of Christ— was not fully satisfied by the central denominational missions model. So, over time, Fairhaven negotiated with the denominational headquarters to receive the denomination's permission to raise up and send some of their own "Fairhaven missionaries." The missions committee was so convinced that the strategy of raising and sending their own would infuse interest and funding into the missions program, they promised that their giving to the central denominational fund would not be hurt—and, in fact, would grow. They were right. Giving to the denomination has gradually increased, and Fairhaven is able to support their own homegrown missionaries, as well as invest in numerous nondenominational missions. In fact Fairhaven Church is one of the major contributing churches to the central CMA missions budget. Beyond that, the missions giving and funding of their own missions program has also increased.

As I travel all over the United States, I have seen very few examples of churches that have been able to work within their own denominational missions agency constraints as well as invest in their homegrown missionaries. I credit the strong leadership direction of Fairhaven Church for their success.

Heart

At the individual level, the heart of the ministry at Fairhaven is a four-step plan that integrates each member into the life, ministry, and commitment of the church. These four steps (without any coaching from me) are called "Running the Bases." Each base moves the member through a step of commitment and covenant.

A base includes classes and electives as well as a demonstration of certain Christian disciplines. Members are challenged with ministry opportunities, responsibilities, care for others in the body, small-group participation, and leadership. Ultimately they are presented with the challenge of a lifestyle committed to the global cause of Christ.

At the conclusion of the members' time at each base, a covenant is agreed on before they move further in their involvement in the church. I am so encouraged by the way the leadership at Fairhaven has implemented this process, especially as it integrates the mandate of missions. What follows are the four covenants.

First Base—The Main Covenant

"To know and worship the God of Glory" is a statement of faith, a statement of belief in the authority of the Word of God, and a statement of commitment to the purpose statement of Fairhaven Church. The first covenant also involves participation in a small group (a hallmark of the Fairhaven Church) and taking a course called Class 201.

Second Base—The Maturity Covenant

"To enable one another to care and grow." This step involves responsibility to the local church through personal discipleship, participation in a small group, witnessing by word and deed, fellowship-group participation, and taking an elective class on finances, on Bible study, or on becoming a contagious Christian.

Third Base—The Ministry Covenant

"To train and involve people in ministry." At this base a member is challenged to discover his or her spiritual gifts and ministry abilities and then serve in an area that best uses his or her gifts. Members are to serve in the church and be available for leadership training. They are to cooperate with other ministries in the church, looking at the needs of the whole body, not just their own ministry in particular. They are to "seek to integrate the priorities of

Christ's global cause into their lifestyle by advancing to the next level of discipleship making." During this time they are to be apprentice disciplers, they are to train and apprentice as a small-group leader, seek a place of service, take electives, and attend a class leading to the final base.

Home Plate—The Missions Covenant

"To speak and live out the gospel and to recruit and send laborers into the world." This base includes the following covenant statement:

> As I continue in my pursuit of Christian maturity and in my service and ministry within the body of Christ, I further commit to developing a lifestyle where Christ's global cause will become the integrating, overriding priority of my life. I will do this by: (1) Being outward focused by looking beyond the boundaries of my life and the life of Fairhaven Church, to the needs of others and the issues confronting our community and world and doing what I can to make a difference for the glory of God. (2) Giving sacrificially of my wealth to community outreach and the cause of world evangelization. (3) Praying for the work of reaching for Christ the people of my community and the peoples of the world. (4) Having a willingness for myself and family members to go wherever God may lead us for the building of the Kingdom of God. I do this recognizing that world evangelization should be a team undertaking involving Fairhaven Church and all believers and extending to all areas of the world including the least reached people groups.

A further aspect of home plate is participating on an International Ministries Regional Team.

At present there are five International Ministries Regional Teams. They are the Africa Team, Asia Team, Europe Team, South America Team, and North America Team. A team consists of the international ministries pastor, the leader of that particular International Ministries Regional Team, missions interns, missionaries in residence when available, and members who are committed to support and promote missions activities and missionaries in that area of the world. Beyond creating awareness and understanding about their particular region of the world, IMTs are to seek to "enlist men and women to be strategically placed in the world in order to reach unreached people." They are also to "contribute to the planting, growth and development of the national church, to underwrite those going into full-time Christian work through encouragement and financial support." There are sixteen specific objectives for each IMT that encompass all areas of missions initiative and education.

Help

The Running the Bases model is effective in assimilating all members into the life of the church and moving them toward becoming world Christians. My evaluation is that Fairhaven has one of the most holistic and integrated missions philosophies going. To provide missions opportunities for every member of the congregation, extensive plans must be in place. Here are some highlights of the missions strategies at Fairhaven.

1. The Multi-National Church Network (MCN) is a program to connect local churches with other "like-minded" churches on the six continents. The purpose is "to broaden the concept of the church and its missions in the minds of each congregation by being in touch with other national churches and leaders on all the continents, developing a practical concept of 'Partnership in Mission' leading to the

development of world Christians." The goal is to have at least one church on each continent with a maximum of eight churches in the network. So a church in Asia can share an idea with a church in South America, or Fairhaven can give some help to a church in Europe.

2. Fairhaven is taking the lead in the region in nurturing missions on an interchurch basis through the Fellowship of Dayton Area Church Missions Committees (FDACMC).

3. Missions education for children and families is integrated into all the ministries of the church, including small groups; Sunday school; youth, men's and women's ministries; and leadership development.

4. Short-term missions programs are in progress year-round.

5. Fairhaven has adopted an unreached people group.

6. Maybe the most important thing that goes on in missions, and in all aspects of church life at Fairhaven, is leadership development. Pete loves his ministry team. At the core of his heart is his desire to raise up leaders who will run with the vision. He plays with his team. Sometimes "business meetings" are just fun and games—with a purpose. He meets with them often, prays with them, challenges them to stretch, and builds them up.

My Call

If Babe Ruth is correct that a winning team is not a bunch of "stars" but players that work together as a team, then Fairhaven has a winning team. Their wisdom not only to work within their denomination but also to build the local body has made them a model to be watched.

Lakeview Baptist Church

1600 E. Glenn Avenue
Auburn, AL 36830
Senior Pastor: Al Jackson
Minister of Missions
and Administration:
John R. West

Another church accepting the challenge of being in a strong missions-oriented denomination with a central missions fund, yet wanting some local giving-and-sending autonomy is Lakeview Baptist Church in Auburn, Alabama. Lakeview is a member of the Southern Baptist Convention. John West, Lakeview's minister of missions, is a straight shooter who doesn't mind telling the truth about the opportunities of being part of a large denominational structure. John notes that the approximately forty thousand Southern Baptist churches include around sixteen million members. These forty thousand churches send about five thousand missionaries through the International Mission Board of the Southern Baptist Convention. That is one missionary for every eight churches. While the International Mission Board is the largest denominational missionary-sending organization, just think what kind of impact it could have internationally if each one of the forty thousand churches sent just one missionary!

John believes the main reason this has not happened is that local church leadership has yet to take its rightful place of ownership in world missions. He goes on to say that Lakeview Baptist Church is so involved in missions because of Pastor Al Jackson.

Heart

Brother Al, as he is known, has a heart and passion for missions locally, nationally, and internationally. John says,

"If it were not for Brother Al's missions heart, I would not have a ministry here."

Under this motivated leadership and the commitment to missions from the pulpit, Lakeview's giving to missions causes has grown from fourteen thousand dollars in 1978 when Brother Al arrived, to almost seven hundred thousand dollars this year! That's 25 percent of the church's total giving. Add to this the facts that there are sixty-one Lakeview members serving internationally and a growing number of Lakeview members are going on national and international mission trips.

To put this all in perspective, John explains, "The 2001 goal for the International Mission Board's Lottie Moon Christmas Offering for International Missions is 115 million dollars. This works out to just over seven dollars a year or two cents a day for every Southern Baptist to reach the world for Jesus! While I am excited about the total offering, the amount given per church member is sad—no, it's pathetic."

Lakeview has made a strategic decision to support missions financially by committing 21 percent of their budget income to both national and international missions causes. This does not include the administrative costs of their missions ministry or their annual International Missions Festival. They are further committed to continually presenting the opportunity for Lakeview's membership to serve both short- and long-term in missions work.

As I look at the numbers, I have to say that Lakeview has made the right decision. Brothers Al and John make a strong case for local church autonomy in the area of missionary recruitment.

Lakeview had a couple of Auburn University students as members who finished their degrees and then married. During their time in Auburn, they were called to missions. Before going overseas, the couple felt they needed to work a few years in the States. They found jobs in South Carolina where they joined a local Southern Baptist church that was 148 years old. While the couple was called to missions at Lakeview, they were the first missionaries ever sent from the South Carolina church in its 148-year history! John says, "Sadly this is the norm in Southern Baptist life, not the exception. Southern Baptist pastors need to keep the missions challenge before their people throughout the year.

"In February 1999 Brother Al challenged our Lakeview Family of Faith to prayerfully consider giving one week's salary to the Lottie Moon Christmas Offering for International Missions that coming December. That year Lakeview gave a record 114,876 dollars in the offering!

"The pastor is the key. He must be the missions mobilizer in the local church," John said. "Brother Al loves to have missionaries share testimonies in Lakeview's worship services as a way of encouraging the congregation to consider missions. If one of our Lakeview missionaries is within fifty miles, Brother Al wants him or her to share."

In fact the missions statement of the church reads, "We believe that God's purpose for Lakeview Baptist Church is to love the Lord God and to express that love by making, nurturing, and equipping disciples of Jesus Christ in Auburn and throughout the world."

Help

John West believes there are at least four factors involved in Lakeview's being a missions-focused church:

1. *The pastor is the leader and promoter.* The leader must be absolutely motivated to keep missions before the people

on a weekly basis. Missions must be in front of the church every Sunday. The International Mission Board of the Southern Baptist Convention provides excellent, professionally made, short video mission updates, tailored for children, students, and adults. Lakeview uses these frequently in their worship and prayer services as well as in their children's and student ministries. Brother Al regularly keeps the call to missions before the people by reminding the Lakeview family of the many opportunities to serve Jesus in "Auburn and throughout the world."

2. Every member is asked to consider short-term missions trip opportunities. Missions trip opportunities are ongoing and it is the desire of the church leadership that every member serve on a missions trip at least once. Each person who serves must recruit between ten and twenty prayer partners and provide an accountability list to John. A ten-person mission team will have between one hundred and two hundred people praying for the team. This broadens the church involvement in missions. Each team member is asked to share prayer requests with his or her prayer partners before the trip, communicate with the prayer partners during the trip, and report to them when they return home. This generates a lot of missions prayer and energy in the church.

3. The church's annual International Missions Festival energizes leadership. In addition to the usual missions conference program, Lakeview has a time when the church leadership—both professional and lay—meets for a banquet with the missions speaker before the conference begins. This time is used to energize the leadership to fully participate in the conference. Local pastors have also been encouraged to attend this banquet in an effort to build local interest and cooperation in missions.

4. Church member ownership is encouraged. Lakeview's Sunday school classes have adopted the church's sixty-one missionaries serving around the world. The classes communicate directly with the missionaries so they can pray effectively for them, minister to their personal needs, learn about their unreached people group ministry, and eventually be the core of a missions team serving with the missionary.

My Call

When I am with John West, I am so encouraged about Lakeview as a model for churches that want to push the edge of the envelope, as far as denominational missions is concerned. The reality that needs to be faced is that this has to come from the pastor and the leadership. Lakeview's carefully designed strategy and amicable relationship with the International Mission Board of the Southern Baptist Convention work well. Both organizations have benefited as far as I can tell.

I challenge churches within denominational structures to think creatively about how to continue to be a part of the larger sending agency and at the same time mobilize and send their own missionaries. Lakeview and Fairhaven are examples of how it can be done in such a way that everybody wins!

8

THE THINKING MAN'S GAME

Xenos Christian Fellowship

1340 Community Park Drive
Columbus, OH 43229
Senior Pastor: Dennis McCallum
Coordinator of Missions Division:
Dave Merker
Director of Missions Mobilization:
Holly McCallum
World Missions Director:
Mark Avers

Hank Aaron holds more Major League batting records than any other player in history. Aaron thought about baseball all the time. He said, "Baseball is a twenty-four-hour job for me." He could tell you anything about the whole season—whom he hit against, whom he got the hits off and during which inning. He played a thinking man's game that lasted all year long.

One of the greatest—and worst—times of Hank Aaron's career was when he broke Babe Ruth's home run record. Fans who had worshiped the Babe were incensed that anyone, much less a Black man, would break Ruth's record. Hank Aaron received hate mail and jeers along with acclaim and cheers. He was a great man whose greatness was refined through adversity.

Hank Aaron was thinking about his game seven days a week—whether he was playing or not. Xenos Christian Fellowship is like Hank Aaron in that way. The leadership team at Xenos is committed to keeping the congregation thinking. That has made it one of the top missions churches in America today.

History

Xenos Christian Fellowship actually began on the campus of Ohio State University as a radical response to the youth and ideological revolution taking place on campuses all across America in the 60s. As Holly McCallum, the director of Missions Mobilization at Xenos, says in an article in *Mobilizer* (vol. 10, no. 2, p. 23):

> . . . from the very beginning we were shaped by our radical redemption out of the disillusionment of the 60s. Our founders' first response was to reach their friends—the unchurched—for Christ. From the start we were taught to focus on others and to be culturally sensitive and relevant. We came to Christ with varying degrees of damage from the world. . . . Though from the beginning we valued missions, this did not immediately translate into action overseas. Because of rapid growth and lack of funds, we were occupied with local training and ministry, particularly evangelism.

In 1982 Xenos decided to hold a Perspectives course. Ralph Winter, founder of the U.S. Center for World Mission, came to Xenos to teach the course, and the resulting excitement and interest in missions changed the church forever. But some hard lessons still had to be learned.

Holly McCallum reports:

In 1985 we sent our first missionary team to Brazil, supporting them 100 percent. In retrospect, we realize they were poorly trained and under-supported in terms of prayer and personal care. The attrition rate was extremely high. . . . This caused us to rethink our missions strategy.

In 1992 Xenos made a strategic decision to form a partnership with one missions agency, World Team. Within a year they sent a new team to Southeast Asia. From lessons learned and mistakes made, these new team members went out better equipped through training, planning, support raising, and the development of a home support team.

Stats

Sunday attendance: 3,700 adults

Missions budget: 1.4 million dollars

Missions staff: 3.8

Number of missionaries sent from local church: 31 in last ten years; 14 in preparation

Most valuable missions agency: World Team (almost exclusively)

As of this year, the missions team is working effectively and strategically in a very difficult area of Southeast Asia. Thirty-one missionaries have been sent to seven fields and fourteen others are in training and preparation to go.

A couple of years ago, I first became involved with Xenos when the missions committee came to an ACMC conference. The church had 3,700 in attendance on Sundays, giving was increasing, and the committee sensed a need to narrow their missions focus. After that ACMC conference, I was asked to do some consulting work with the committee. As a result of those consultations, Xenos has reorganized their missions staff and focus into two initiatives: Their "Mobilization Department exists to glorify God by motivating servants to become more aware and involved in missions." The "World Missions Department exists to glorify God by sending and caring for missions teams overseas" (*Mobilizer,* vol. 10, no. 2, p. 24).

I also encouraged Xenos to do one or two things well rather than try to do everything and then not do anything very well. I am convinced that any church that makes a strategic decision to do one or two things well, and not worry about trying to do everything, will see great results. Xenos, as well as most of the churches in this book, is living proof of that conviction.

So there were three significant decisions in the maturing of missions mobilization at Xenos: (1) the decision to host a Perspectives course, (2) the decision to recruit and partner with one mission agency—WorldTeam, and (3) the decision to attend an ACMC conference and as a follow-up to have a consultant come and help them narrow their focus.

Heart

Xenos began as a cell-church movement and has remained faithful to that original purpose. At present there are more than 150 home groups and 300 cell groups in the church, representing about 85 percent of the total community. Gary DeLashmutt, one of the senior pastors, says, "Xenos is not a large-meeting church that happens to have home groups. It is a home group–based church that also has large meetings."

There are three different kinds of home groups, each with unique purposes. (1) Home churches are groups of twenty-five to sixty people who meet for discussions, teaching, and social times. These groups are open to non-Christians. (2) Small groups are groups of ten to twenty, led by lay leaders, that offer Bible teaching and discussions of deeper issues. (3) Ministry Teams are like small groups but the members are usually working in a common ministry so this can be a time for team building and prayer for the ministry.

The idea of small groups has impacted mission strategy at Xenos as well. Missionary candidates are expected to develop home support teams—groups committed to the physical and spiritual support of the missionary. Each home group has a missions representative who provides information and communication between the home group and the missionary.

When missionaries arrive on the field, they become part of a team that has been sent out by Xenos. The model for small groups that is experienced at Xenos is carried over to the mission field. It becomes a natural way to do ministry in a cross-cultural context and provides ministry stability for missionaries.

Help

Here are some strategies that have been pivotal in turning Xenos into a missions-mobilized church.

Mobilizing through missionary accreditation. Based on the missions strategy and policies, Xenos places their missionaries in three categories: (a) well-wishers (nonpriority, have the blessing of the church but no supervision or support); (b) assisted (nonpriority but missionaries are qualified and can raise a negotiated amount of support from the church); and (c) fully accredited (priority ministries and fully qualified personnel. In most cases 70–80 percent of their support will come from Xenos. They have the church's undivided attention and are promoted and cared for).

Xenos has developed a fine set of qualifications for missionary accreditation that I think could be a model for many churches. All the concepts are not transferrable, but it sets an excellent standard. Here are those standards:

Candidates must be members of the Servant Team, which means they have been through the theological and practical ministry classes, give at least 5 percent of their gross income to Xenos, and have a proved ministry track record within home group ministries. This usually means they have successfully planted and led home groups. In addition to this, their character must be exemplary and they must meet the World Team testing, interviews, and assessments. Formal applications and ministry plans must be filed with both Xenos and World Team. Final decisions are made jointly with Xenos and World Team. All accredited missionaries are required to have a home support team. They must be willing to submit to periodic reviews and evaluations and they must work from their approved ministry plan. Each missionary then signs a "Memo of Understanding," which serves as an agreement between them and Xenos.

This is a very carefully defined and executed part of Xenos's missions ministry and is the result of lessons learned early on in the life of the church.

Mobilizing through education. Xenos has done a thoughtful job of mobilizing a thinking congregation. They have a program called Missions Mobilizers that is designed to get everyone "aware and involved." Early on in their time at Xenos, people sign up for two awareness and two involvement activities. These commitments are tracked in a database. When members have gone through these programs, they receive certain benefits. They receive a special Passport newsletter, discounts on books, and discounts on Xenos-sponsored conferences. The mobilization department has developed an excellent web site that keeps current missions information available to everyone in the church.

Mobilizing through small groups. Recently the elders felt they were having too many meetings and consuming too much of their staff's and volunteers' time. Xenos has decided to cut back on fellowship-wide events and revitalize their cell-based philosophy. This is a challenge for missions mobilization, but Holly McCallum and the team are up to the task. The missions rep in each cell group has become the strategic link for communication between missions and the group. They are working to equip and motivate these reps to tailor missions to their particular group and ministry. Because large gatherings will be less frequent, any missions emphasis must be powerful and pack a punch within the time given.

Xenos makes good use of their home group missions representatives. These reps communicate missions material to their home groups, make sure missionaries visit home groups when they are home, and let the home groups know of opportunities for involvement and support in the lives of the missionaries. The members of the home groups are encouraged to go on short-term trips to visit and help out the missionaries they pray for and support. A close bond grows between the missionary and the small group that supports and prays for him or her.

One or more of the senior pastors visits all missionaries at least once every two years. Missions is emphasized from the pulpit and at special church gatherings. In the regular curriculum of the church, there is a basic introduction to missions class and a short-term–missions class. The Xenos leadership considers "equipping ministries" one of their strengths and this equipping is central to the training and sending of their own missionaries. They have set up a seminary-level, missions-specific seminar for missions candidates. Xenos regularly hosts a Perspectives course or is involved with courses that are taught in the area.

Mobilizing for missions through the study center. Xenos maintains a collection of more than 5,000 books, 2,300 documents, and more than 6,000 tapes and videos. The study center library has powerful personal computers for church member use and is open almost every day until 11 P.M. The availability of good information on world evangelization is a service to the church that raises awareness and involvement in missions. I would encourage churches to find the space and resources to make quality libraries and study centers available to their people. There are valuable missions resources available to churches that just cannot be found in the local Christian bookstore.

Mobilizing for missions giving. One of the most unusual events in missions giving that I am aware of takes place at the Xenos Christian Fellowship annual Fiscal Support Team (FST) retreat. Once a year the Fiscal Support Team (giving members of the church) meet to vote on budget modules. The results of the voting have a significant impact on how the church allocates money to ministries, and therefore, by design, which ministries become priorities.

The retreat begins with the senior pastors' reviewing what God has done at the church in the past year, and then there is a time of vision setting for the future. Some voting is done on one-time projects like new facilities, but the "fun" begins on Saturday when each of the seven administrative divisions that make up Xenos's organizational structure give their presentations. The divisions are Pastoral, Missions, Student Ministries, Equipping, Operations, Community Relations, and Quality Initiatives. Each division presents a proposal that is beyond its base budget, which has already been set by the elders and management. The FST hears these presentations and votes on which ones will receive the extra funding they request. Like a faith promise budget, the money is designated by faith when it is greater than the budget of the present year. This means that critical decisions will be made about the next year of ministry through the voting of the FST.

In a congenial effort to get the FST to vote for their funding needs, the divisions do elaborate presentations through power point, multi-media overhead presentations, and whatever marketing tools they can utilize to convince the FST to vote for their projects. After a day, which sounds like a national political convention, the votes are in and the tallies made. For the past five years Missions and Student

Ministries have received the highest increases in support, clearly communicating how highly they are valued. As I see it, not only does missions get a good opportunity to be funded well, the intensity and exposure at an event like the fiscal retreat can only serve to raise the awareness and urgency of supporting missions in the church.

Mobilizing through partnership. Xenos Christian Fellowship is thirty years old. About eight years ago, after some difficult years with sending out unprepared missionaries, Xenos made the decision to find and work with one main mission agency for the selecting and training of missionaries. They looked for an agency that could help them with training and preparation as well as on-the-field supervision and evaluation. They also decided that their strategy would be to concentrate on church planting. That year a partnership was drawn up between Xenos Christian Fellowship and World Team.

The purpose statement of the partnership states that it would "exist to jointly send and support church planting teams to selected unreached urban centers or people groups so that Christ builds multiplying churches among them. The partnership will cooperate in selecting, assessing, training, supporting, deploying, coaching, and managing the church planting teams." The partnership laid out the particular responsibilities of the church and the mission in areas of policy, selecting team members and a team leader, training and coaching, financial responsibilities, decision making, and conflict resolution. The results of this liaison over the past years have been very encouraging, certainly enough to interest other churches in attempting a similar model.

Xenos is working on sending eight families to the field in 2001. Five couples will join the existing fields and three couples will open a new ministry in Cambodia. All of these teams will go with World Team.

Mobilizing for missions through care. The world ministries director at Xenos, Mark Avers, is working hard to increase the effectiveness of the church's missionary care. Mark spoke at Urbana 2000 on this and other aspects of the missions strategy at Xenos. The people of Xenos never sit back and let the status quo kick in. The ethos is always to keep thinking and working to do better.

My Call

Xenos Christian Fellowship is certainly not a stereotypical church. Its birth on the campus of Ohio State and its commitment to small home groups and to growing up a thinking laity set it apart. What has excited me is their desire to put world missions into that mix, and do it in a way that is an authentic expression and outcome of the particular culture at Xenos. The church, which is largely Gen-Xers and boomers (very few over fifty), has embraced missions wholeheartedly. I believe one of the reasons for this is the regular exposure to missions and missionaries they receive in the small groups.

Sunday is a worship and teaching day at Xenos, but body life and missions awareness go on in small groups. Xenos offers an exciting model for young, small group–based churches. I regard highly their missionary accreditation process, which is tough, but also built into the whole mindset and lifestyle at Xenos.

This is a church with models that can be followed. Their web site www.xenos.org is worth a visit.

9

PITCHER

HURLING SOME HEAT AT HOME

University Presbyterian Church

4540 15th Avenue NE
Seattle, WA 98105
Senior Pastor: Dr. Earl Palmer
Pastor of Global Mission:
   Ken Kierstead

When I was a kid, I wasn't allowed to play baseball or go to baseball games on Sunday. But often my brother and I managed to sneak out our bedroom window and squeeze through the fence of the great Connie Mack Stadium and for a few hours soak in the wonder of Major League Baseball.

Connie Mack was the manager of the Philadelphia A's for fifty years. He was a legend, and to us kids, whatever he said was gospel truth.

Connie Mack said that Christy Mathewson was the greatest pitcher that ever lived. He was the first great superstar of the twentieth century. And I believe him. In the 1905 World Series "Matty" did the unthinkable—he pitched three complete shut-out victories for the New York Giants and won the series. Christy Mathewson brought something to the game that no one else, not Ty Cobb or even Babe Ruth, could bring—a certain touch of class.

Ray Robinson, Mathewson's biographer wrote, "He defined baseball in a new and acceptable way for millions with his brain (a Bucknell student who was class president), demeanor, personality and great achievement on the field. He was the first authentic sports hero and he lived up to his popular image" (Ray Robinson, *Matty: An American Hero—Christy Mathewson of the New York Giants* [Oxford University Press, 1994]).

In 1908 Matty had his best year, winning thirty-seven games, one of the best records in baseball history. It was that same year, one block from the University of Washington, that a small church was planted in Seattle, University Presbyterian Church (UPC).

History

Although UPC was planted in 1908, it was not until 1977 that a full-time missions pastor was hired. Until then, missions had been the domain of a few "missions professionals" and not embraced by the whole congregation. The leadership challenged missions pastor Tim Dearborn to "move missions from the periphery to the heart of UPC, from being the concern of a highly committed few to the vision of everyone" (from the church's missions perspectus, "God's Love Revealed"). Senior Pastor Bruce Larson, who arrived in 1980, energized the congregation to "go for it" in missions. His enthusiasm was fired by travel overseas. In June of 1983 Bruce Larson said to the church, "What would it look like if one church was totally mobilized for world missions?" At that time the budget for missions was 143,000 dollars. Sixteen years later the mission budget is 1.8 million dollars and there are 78 missionaries and more than 700 serving as missions volunteers.

In 1985 Art Beals, who had recently resigned as president of World Concern International, took over the position of missions pastor. Later, Dr. Earl Palmer, who is known nationally for his commitment to preaching and sound biblical exposition, became the senior pastor at UPC. But during these years as Art traveled all over the world and brought the excitement of missions to the church, he felt the church had more to give. He described a defining moment in his own life and in the life of the church:

Stats

Sunday attendance: 5,000

Missions income as part of total budget: 1.8 million dollars of 8.7 million dollars

Number of missionaries from church: 78 fully supported

Missions staff: 18

Most valuable missions agencies:

World Concern

YWAM

InterVarsity/IFES

"One Sunday I was preaching at all five services during the day and a funny thing happens when you've been preaching for more than forty years; it's fresh material, but you have so many years of experience and sometimes you almost enter into a dialogue with God when you are preaching, and God brings something to your own attention out of your sermon.

"So I was preaching but I remember I kind of did a play off Martin Luther King's 'I Have a Dream.' And instead of saying, 'I have a dream,' I was saying, 'I have a vision.' And all of a sudden the Holy Spirit interrupted me. Now, I never stopped the sermon, but the Spirit said, 'How dare you tell these people you have a vision! Don't you realize that today you are preaching to more than five thousand people here at the church as well as thousands more on the radio? Don't you realize that they've got far more vision and more dreams than you will ever have? Why don't you quit putting your visions forth and find ways to help the laypeople dream their dreams and put their visions forth?'

"And that was the single most pivotal point in ministry for me."

Art Beals explains that what developed from that time in the missions history at UPC was a whole new approach to missions in the church that really had to do with leadership. He calls it bottom-up instead of top-down leadership.

Art feels that much of the evangelical establishment in missions today is very much tied to strategy. People are sent to ACMC and other missions conferences and they come home armed with the latest strategy to implement at their church. Sometimes it's the 10/40 window, or unreached people groups, or adopting a people, or leadership, and so on. Art says that none of this is bad but wonders if these strategies are where the people are. Leaders come back from conferences and lay their dreams on the congregation. That's top-down. "There will always be people who will follow the dream—they are the followers," says Art. "But we need to tap the resources of the people who have their own dreams. Then and there I decided that none of my staff, including myself would *EVER* start anything. If it didn't start with people who were committed to making it happen, then we didn't want to do it."

Since 1993 Art Beals has served concurrently as the missions specialist and partnership facilitator with the Presbyterian Church–USA for southeastern Europe, Turkey, and the Caucasus. However, University Presbyterian Church's missions vision, under the leadership of Ken Kierstead, who served for some years as Art Beals's associate, has continued its commitment to bottom-up missions.

Heart

UPC continues to be innovative and intentional when it comes to their missions program. Here are some of their ideas that challenge my thinking.

Bottom-up! mobilization. Here's an example of how bottom-up mobilization works: A church member from UPC travels to Romania when it is first opened to tourists. The church member sees the hundreds of neglected orphans there and feels burdened about the situation. She comes back to the church and tells Ken, "We've got to do something about the orphans in Romania!" Ken says, "Well, what is God telling you to do?" He prays with the person and advises her to gather a group of people who know her and share the vision. This person should find other people in the church who are concerned about orphans. They should pray that God would help them bring together a task force of like-minded members committed to the same concern.

There is no manual for what a task force should be or do. That makes some people frustrated, but the leadership believes that the day you organize what a task force is will be the day you take the fire away. Presently there are about forty task forces operating. They report to the missions office and are accountable for what they are doing. Task forces live and die, some finish their task, and new ones are born. This is exactly what UPC expects. A task force usually has from eight to twenty-five people who have a single missions vision that God has laid on their hearts.

Give missions away! The purpose of the staff in the missions department is to pastor and mentor the laity who are doing the work of missions. They are not there to try to mobilize the laity to do something the leadership wants; they are there to empower and minister to the laity. Presently eighteen full- and part-time staff are supporting and enabling around seven hundred lay volunteers' efforts all over the world. There are Price Waterhouse financiers teaching stock brokers in Kyrgyzstan; some of UPC's 177 medical doctors are serving on all the continents; students are attending university in Kosovo and Albania, building relationships with the future leaders of those countries; churches are being planted in Africa; and leprosy clinics are being served in Nepal. Dozens of other creative ministries have been born through the vision of laypeople in the church.

As I look at this model, I realize the tremendous effort needed to encourage, train, and facilitate ministry teams that are regularly coming to and going from the church. Bottom-up doesn't mean freedom to do whatever you want. So the need for a large staff to empower and manage people in ministry is necessary. The missions pastor's most important job is to mobilize the laity and put missions into their hands and hearts. The number one responsibility on the missions pastor's job description at UPC is to "give missions away." I like that.

Open the floodgates of generosity. Art Beals used to say, "People commit themselves and give most to that which they were part of creating." This is the philosophy at UPC. The leadership believes that if you allow the laity to create ministry, the money will flow. Since there are several score of fully supported missionaries and many more partially funded missionaries from UPC today, and each missionary has a support team, there are hundreds of "fund raisers" within the congregation. So the result is that there are no faith promise or fund-raising drives for missions. When you go from bottom up, you get the dream first, the task force is formed, and then the idea goes to the leadership (elders and staff). When the leaders see that a proposal has the mark of God's blessing on it, they say, "Go do it!" Then the designated giving comes. Right now, it is at least 1.8 million dollars in dreams!

It's not exactly orthodox, but I can't argue with what works.

Small groups relate! Bruce Larson came to UPC as the senior pastor in 1980. In the evangelical community he is known for his relational theology, and the church was well taught in the area of community and mutual care in the biblical context. But back in 1970 God had already begun the ministry of small groups at UPC. A laywoman in the church, Roberta Hestenes, whose husband was on the faculty at the University of Washington, had a vision for what small groups could do for the church.

Today they say that if you're not in a small group, you have to be hiding. Otherwise, it's impossible. If you attend UPC, you're in a small group. That's all there is to it! Small groups often become missions or ministry task forces. An example is Project Farewell.

About five years ago a group approached the missions staff. Included in the group were the chief news anchor of the ABC Seattle affiliate, a prominent Chinese-American lawyer in the city, chairman of the board of the Nordstrom Corporation, chairman of the board of the Washington Athletic Club, a professional baseball player, and their wives. So it was a high-powered group. They were concerned about single moms on welfare.

The group met with Senior Pastor Earl Palmer and Art Beals, who was missions pastor at the time. They shared their dream. Earl asked Art what he thought, and Art realized that it would take a vast mobilization of the laity to care for these women. The small group was proposing care groups of five to ten couples to come around each single mom on welfare. It was a dream. They wanted to figure out how to transition a woman from welfare to work within six months and stand by that woman in an intensive way the whole time. They agreed that they wouldn't touch the program unless they could hire a full-time professional to take charge. They were told they had two weeks to find a professional who would run the program. It was back in the laity's hands.

Well, that group believed this was their call of God, and it happened. UPC now has Project Farewell—"Say farewell to welfare." Dan Wilson, the catcher for the Seattle Mariners, and his wife, Annie, are two of the most compassionate care-group leaders the program has. UPC has prioritized Project Farewell and the laity has embraced it wholeheartedly.

Another example is the Albania Task Force. In 1986 a member of the congregation had a son who was studying in Sweden. While he was there, he got this "crazy idea" that God wanted him to be a missionary to Albania. Albania was closed. His mom shared the idea with the missions pastor and they came up with a plan. Her son would go to university at Kosovo and learn the language and be ready when Albania was opened. She gathered her task force and they began to pray. This was before the problems began in Bosnia. By the time the war had begun, God had in place a group on the ground who could minister effectively.

Bottom-up, relational, and generous small groups and task forces are what make the missions expansion at UPC a reality. It takes a certain kind of leadership to make it possible. It's a model that has aspects that could be incorporated into many church missions strategies, but it's not for everyone.

Help

Last year the leadership at UPC published a booklet highlighting the faithfulness of God in the ninety years of missions ministry at the church. As I flipped through the pages, I became aware of numerous ways that the programs and initiatives could be a model to others. Here are a few ideas that are working well at UPC.

World deputation. This is a scholarship opportunity UPC provides for university students to go on short-term missions trips. Since the program began in 1953, more than eight hundred students have participated in the program. Many have become missionaries and pastors or gone into full-time ministry as a result of their missions experience.

Intentional communities. With a focus on lifestyle ministry, the Intentional Community (IC) program is committed to learning about life in community and in the city. Participants agree to minister with an established urban ministry for at least ten hours a week and meet with the IC facilitator to eat and pray together at least once a week. Through its members, the IC program provides at least nine thousand hours each year to urban ministries in the city of Seattle. At the center of the program, the focus is Jesus Christ and the work of the kingdom. Through shared experiences in the city context, participants learn how to balance their faith with serving the poor and pursuing Christian community. Those who come through the program say it is "in your face" accountability, great training for intercultural missions.

TWAD. Travel With a Difference is designed to awaken and deepen a traveler's understanding of what ministries are going on as an extension of UPC. Travelers come home knowing better how to pray for missionaries and the world.

Journey. Journey is usually a two-week short ministry experience to give members an opportunity for cross-cultural service. The joke at UPC is "When God wants to teach you something, he takes you on a trip." The leadership has a long-term goal that every member of UPC will eventually have an opportunity to go on a journey overseas to experience the spiritual growth and renewal that can result.

Ethnic church partners. UPC has had an opportunity to do missions right in their own city. They have planted a number of ethnic churches and have seen them become self-supporting, calling their own pastors. Four such churches are the Khmer Evangelical Church (Cambodian), Bethel Ethiopian Church, Ekklesia Indonesian Evangelical Church, and the Persian Evangelical Church of the Good Shepherd. These churches first met at UPC but then were able, often through the help of UPC task forces, to acquire their own facilities. Experiences with short-term missions overseas has brought members back ready to find international friends in their own backyard.

Missionary care. As the number of missionaries grew it became too difficult for the missions staff alone to adequately care for them. The Barnabas Ministry was created about ten years ago to mobilize the laity to participate in missionary care. Each missionary is asked to select someone in the congregation who knows him or her well and would be an advocate and representative. This Barnabas minister maintains close communication with the missionary and is a liaison with the global ministries staff at UPC. After selection, Barnabas ministers are trained. There is now an excellent and very extensive manual to help Barnabas ministers with any concerns. The Barnabas minister focuses on three aspects of the missionary's life—preparing to leave, serving cross-culturally, and reentry back home. A global care coordinator was hired to oversee and expand this ministry.

UPC scholars. This is a scholarship program designed to help international students studying in the United States or abroad who intend to go into full-time ministry. UPC wants to come alongside these future leaders and work toward helping them reach their ministry goals.

Global task forces. Members who have a particular burden for or interest in a certain area of the world or ministry are encouraged and helped to be active, praying task forces. They encourage missionaries and make visible to the rest of the church the needs and initiatives in that area of the world. Many global task forces are already operating successfully. These groups have three goals: build relationships, mobilize resources, and support projects.

There are also global prayer groups that focus strategically on praying for certain areas of the world.

A new model for missions. As a result of UPC's intense involvement in Albania, a story that could take a whole book to tell, they have developed a set of principles for strategic missions. They say these principles are evolving, but this is what they have begun to use to shape their mission:

1. *Begin with lay vision.* A couple, John and Lynne Quanrud, came to the UPC leadership and sought their support for a calling to know and serve the Albanian people in Kosovo, even before westerners were allowed to enter Albania. They were among the first Western missionaries allowed to enter Albania when it opened up in 1991. Today Emmanual Church in Tirana is UPC's sister church in Albania.

2. *See what God has been doing before we arrived.* A tiny remnant of Albanian Christians were found. Some young people, now college age, began a college ministry with John and Lynne.

3. *Start with what we can do best.* University students who had been in UPC University Ministries program went to Albania to pioneer Bible studies and develop relationships with students. UPC professionals went to help the new nation with law, business, health, and education.

4. *Respect preexisting Christian ministries.* UPC has sought to cooperate and encourage the Orthodox Church in Albania.

5. *Empower local leadership.* Much of UPC's financial and prayer support now goes to Albanian national leaders, whose faith and training have been nurtured by UPC missionaries.

6. *Expect the unexpected.* "If the missions department had worked out a 10-year strategic plan for world mission in 1990, Albania would not have been in it. Yet UPC and the Quanruds were ready to move when the borders opened. In less than a decade, 23 UPCers have served for one or more years. Scores more have visited, served short term, prayed, and donated to a ministry that began outside the core budget and now adds up to well over half a million dollars....When warfare over Kosovo unleashed a flood of refugees on the impoverished Albanians in the spring of 1999, UPC personnel were there. Art Beals coordinated the denomination's response to the crisis, working with both the evangelical churches and the Albanian Orthodox Church. UPC responded generously. The missions department received one of the largest single crisis-response offerings ever in addition to countless offers from the congregation to help. Through this model, Albania has truly become part of UPC" (from the missions report).

My Call

Like a good baseball manager, you can sift through this chapter as you would a game strategy book. Not every play will work for your team, but there are lots of ideas and plays to consider. See what works for you and go and get into the game. UPC is a huge church, but there are principles here that can work for any size church. They took a long time to get to this point, so don't despair if you're not in the World Series yet.

10

QUALITIES OF GREAT LEADERSHIP

Wheaton Bible Church

Main Street at Franklin
Wheaton, IL 60187
Senior Pastor: Rob Bugh
Pastor of Cross-Cultural Ministries:
Doug Christgau

**Cedar Springs
Presbyterian Church**

9132 Kingston Pike S.W.
Knoxville, TN 37923-5273
Senior Pastor: John Wood
Missions Pastor: Mac Sells

He said he was tired of yelling at people, so the irascible and colorful Earl Weaver retired in 1982. Even though he was every umpire's nightmare, you couldn't argue with his success. He was ejected from ninety-one games and suspended four times. Yet his aggressiveness wasn't arbitrary; it was very calculated, calculated enough to win him four American League pennants and a World Series. His

121

Major League winning percentage was the third best in history.

Opinionated, disciplined, and raucous, Weaver possessed an insatiable desire to win. His managerial philosophy was to know what each player can do and then get that player to do it at the right time. He said, "They're not all great players but they can all do something well."

The two "managers" of missions that I feel are second to none as missions pastors in America today couldn't be more unlike Weaver in their styles. I guess there are a few ways in which missions doesn't reflect baseball!

Wheaton Bible Church—Pastor Doug Christgau

Doug Christgau is the best missions pastor I've ever met, and you can quote me on that. When Wheaton Bible Church called Doug to be their missions pastor a few years ago, they moved into the major leagues in my book. Previously Doug had been the missions pastor at Black Rock Congregational Church in Fairfield, Connecticut. Doug's creativity and passion had made the missions conference an all-church highlight in the church calendar. Nobody wanted to miss any part of the conference. At Black Rock you marked two things on your calendar at the beginning of the year—Christmas and the missions conference!

So why did Doug come to Wheaton? At Black Rock, missions was just 50 percent of his job description. He wanted to do missions full-time, and Wheaton gave him that opportunity. Doug was also looking forward to working with the new pastor, Rob Bugh. Rob is a force for change, and Doug sensed that the church was on the move.

As I look at Doug Christgau's track record as a missions pastor, I see a number of fundamentals that have guided his ministry. I would like to explore some of these and suggest why they make him a successful missions pastor.

Fundamental 1

Don't lose focus by trying to be "trendy." Doug has been involved in missions for a long time and he is not always convinced that he needs to hop on the latest missions bandwagon. He says, "I love working with traditional missions agencies. I would rather take mature programs and improve on them than throw out the baby with the bathwater because of the latest Barna report. The latest word is that traditional missions don't give you the best 'bang for your buck.' I don't believe that. If you make dollars the highest value in missions strategy, then that's a choice that has been made, but I'm not convinced." He says, "It is estimated that when you put all the costs for buildings, pastors' salaries and housing, radio and TV, promotional materials, and everything together, it costs investments of thousands to get a person saved in Wheaton! Who knows how they figure this all out, but they do. So as I look at it, you can't say that missions, as it operates, is inefficient. I just don't believe it."

Doug admits that he works with a church that has a grand and glorious history in missions and he admires the builders who made it that way. Builders are characterized as faithful givers and prayer warriors. "These people have a heart for missions and I admire them," says Doug. "However, 95 percent of my efforts is invested in making missions relevant to people under fifty, and we are making progress in that regard through personalized prayer part-

Stats

Members: 1,665

Missions budget as percent of total budget: 27 percent

Number of missionaries sent from Wheaton Bible Church: 78 active

Missions staff: 1.5

Most valuable missions agencies:

TEAM

SIM

Frontiers

nerships, contemporary missions festival programming and a great variety of short-term missions trips. We have completely changed the church missions strategy from its glorious historical roots and are taking initiatives to make it work." Doug looks at the system like the excellent manager he is and figures out how to move wisely through change. He doesn't have to hurry because Doug is in this for the long haul.

Fundamental 2

Get as many people overseas as possible—especially the leadership. Doug Christgau is committed to getting the leadership of the church overseas as often as possible. It helps keep the church from being self-focused. Doug says he travels overseas three times a year and spends time living with the missionaries and talking about projects that Wheaton Bible Church supports. You don't have to spend much time with Doug before you realize that he knows about each missionary. He knows their ups and downs, struggles and victories. Because of his regular involvement with missionaries, he feels he has the right to say that they are doing a good job and that the "pundits" who say that 50 percent of the mission force could come home and we'd be the better for it are wrong.

Recently Wheaton Bible Church did an in-depth assessment of all of their ninety-three missionaries. Of that total missionary force, only seven needed change or enforced retirement. Even in the corporate world, those statistics would be good. Doug says, "It's good for Americans to see that our missionaries are not always in the most stimulating environment where they can hear motivational speakers, go to seminars, and get the latest news. They have to be self-motivated and able to sustain things for a long time. We in the West are not good at that."

Fundamental 3

Mobilization of the American church is the most strategic thing we can do in missions. That's a saying of Ralph Winter (founder of the U.S. Center for World Mission), and it keeps Doug challenged. In order to mobilize the church, you need to understand it. Doug says, "The self-centeredness of the American church is a huge concern. The church often denigrates missions because missions becomes competition to its local programs and strategies.

Doug expresses the concern that churches often elevate local evangelism to the level of missions. They think they are doing this for the sake of the lost, but they're doing it for themselves. He says, "What I mean by that is that it is a route to church growth—it's about new carpets! I know of an effective missionary who had his support cut by 60 percent because the church was hiring two new people for local evangelism. But isn't local evangelism the responsibility of every church member? That is what we do! It can become a monument to ourselves.

"I believe we can have a church that is strong in local evangelism and strong in mission. The minister of evangelism here at Wheaton Bible Church is probably my biggest advocate—and I his. These programs *must* be complementary not competitive. That's my concern."

Fundamental 4

Be sure you understand the shifts in missions in North American churches. The missions profile is changing and a wise missions pastor needs to be alert to these trends.

I heartily agree with Doug! The face of missions is changing. What follows is a list of trends that has been developed by ACMC and would make a great discussion outline for your next missions committee retreat!

1. From supporting others—to supporting our own
2. From supporting more missionaries for less—to supporting fewer missionaries for more
3. From delegating to agencies—to doing it ourselves
4. From delegated accountability—to direct accountability
5. From long-term—to short-term
6. From geography—to people groups
7. From going anywhere—to going to centers of influence (cities)
8. From foreign peoples—to unreached peoples
9. From overseas—to here too
10. From sending individuals—to sending teams
11. From supporting North Americans—to supporting nationals
12. From open-ended ventures—to contained (time-limited) ventures
13. From slow progress is okay—to quick wins are desired
14. From a select few involved—to everyone involved
15. From activity—to accomplishment
16. From long-term giving—to seasonal and spontaneous giving
17. From few questions asked—to many questions asked
18. From institutional loyalty—to consumer mentality
19. From "anything goes"—to excellence expected
20. From giving and praying—to giving, praying, and going

I think this list is an excellent summary of where churches are moving. In my travels all over the country I see the importance of missions pastors keeping on the cutting edge of change.

Fundamental 5

Fill your church with many nations and cultures. At any time when you walk into the lobby of the Wheaton Bible Church, you could bump into a Sikh from India, a sheikh from the Middle East, a Cambodian language student, an Hispanic pastor on his way to a meeting with his elders, a Filipino Sunday school teacher ... and the list goes on. Through organizations like SIM and World Relief, Wheaton Bible Church has managed to fill its facilities with ethnic groups from all over the world. The growing Hispanic congregation does joint missions trips with the English congregation and vice versa. Doug Christgau likes it that way. The world is all around the church and so the mission field does not seem so far away.

Stats

Members: 3,300

Home missions budget: $500,000

Overseas missions budget: $1.9 million

Number of home church missionaries sent in last 10 years: 37

Missions staff: 2.5

Most valuable missions agencies: older established agencies

Cedar Springs Presbyterian Church—Pastor Mac Sells

Mac Sells makes you want to be a missions pastor. He loves every missionary family and knows all about their burdens and triumphs. He knows their stories and prays for them faithfully. On the front of the Missionary Candidate Preparation Manual, which Mac has produced, is a very telling quote, written by C. T. Studd, the founder of World-wide Evangelical Crusade (WEC). The quote, written from the Congo, helps you understand Mac:

> Send us people with initiative, who can carry themselves and others too; such as need to be carried hamper the work

and weaken those who should be spending their strength
for the heathen. Weaklings should be nursed at home! If
any have jealousy, pride, or talebearing traits lurking about
them, do not send them, nor any who are prone to criti-
cize. Send only Pauls and Timothys; men who are full of
zeal, holiness and power. All others are hindrances. If you
send us ten such men the work will be done. Quantity is
nothing; quality is what matters.

Those tough words show a passion for missions and for
missions done well. Mac Sells does missions with excellence. There are two on the missions staff at Cedar Springs
Presbyterian Church and one secretary and, as Mac says,
"We are bare bones and work like dogs!"

What is it that Mac Sells believes about missions that makes
him work so hard and be a missions pastor for twenty years?
Well, here are some important things that Mac believes.

Celebrate Missions

Mac Sells believes in celebrating missions in the church.
Cedar Springs still has an eight-day missions conference. He
believes it works because the Gen-Xers, who are the next
generation of leaders at the church, want to come and they
want to give. Last year the elders added five Gen-Xers to
the world missions committee, a committee of twenty-five.
Because the next generation is so committed, because
they've seen God work in missions, Mac sees the annual
missions event as something they will continue to support
for a long time.

Honesty

Mac believes in missionaries getting honest. Mac tells
this story: "Several years ago we learned just before the con-

ference that our plenary speaker was leaving after the Tuesday evening meeting. So we asked three of our missionary couples to take the service and 'get honest' with us—tell us those things that they might not normally say in a formal church setting. What happened was that 'Get Honest Night' was born and became a highlight of the conference. Tears, laughter, and being real are hallmarks of the evening. Our people never want to miss that event. We don't want our missionaries on pedestals or in ivory towers. We love them because they are real—just like us."

Faith Promise Giving

Back in 1974 one of the elders read a book about faith promise. He became so excited about it that he bought the book for every member in the church. That year Cedar Springs adopted the faith promise method of giving. Last year they reached 1.9 million dollars in faith promises. This is completely separate from the general budget. The general budget pays for all home missions and the missions staff salaries as well. Faith promise goes only to overseas missions. This gives the people a connection to the missionaries themselves. When they promise to give, they also promise to pray for a missionary and write to him or her. Each member is assigned a missionary, becomes his or her advocate in a missionary sponsor program, and has responsibilities for that missionary for a whole year. For Mac, Faith Promise is very inclusive. Every year the church has given more than was promised. Cedar Springs has one of the best-run programs that I am aware of.

Prayer

Mac's commitment to prayer requires him to be in communication with all the missionaries on a regular basis. He responds to every letter he receives. If he has not heard from a missionary in three months, he writes to find out what is happening. So prayer is current. The missions committee prays for an hour before every committee meeting, and when there are major decisions to be made, there are regular prayer times in preparation for the decision. Prayer meetings for global missions are going on throughout the week. Preparation for every decision regarding missions is made with serious times of prayer. This bunch really prays!

Senior Pastor Involvement

Mac believes that the senior pastor should be an active member of the missions committee. He says this is absolutely key to the missions vision at the church. Mac feels the strong missions involvement at Cedar Springs ultimately can be attributed to the commitment of the elders to world evangelization and the consistent expository preaching of God's Word from the pulpit. The senior pastor is committed to missions because he travels regularly to visit missionaries and projects the church supports.

Unreached People Groups

Cedar Springs has adopted six different unreached people groups. Mac says this has been a very effective means for developing world Christians at the church. With six groups from different corners of the world, there is always something interesting happening and something to report from one group or the other. This keeps the interest of the congregation piqued. They receive reports weekly about the unreached groups, including information on the people being sent on short-term ministry from Cedar Springs and what they are doing, what projects are being sponsored among the people groups, what contacts are being made, the political scene, and many other updates and prayer reminders.

It took two years of prayer before Cedar Springs was able to adopt these people groups, and then almost another two years before things began to happen, but God has used the church dramatically in the six groups with which they are working. Churches have been planted, schools set up, the Jesus film translated, and a children's Bible published, to name a few.

The Local Church

Mac believes that the local church can make a difference. He tells of the time that twelve thousand dollars was urgently needed to help fund a project in Azerbaijan. When the need was announced in church, one adult Sunday school class asked if they could have the project. Within a few weeks the class had raised the total amount. Mac Sells says people love to give, they love to get involved, and they want to pray. The church wants to be mobilized; it just takes committed people to help make that happen.

I'm with Mac on that.

My Call

Doug Christgau and Mac Sells are exceptional, but I'm sure there are many more like them that I have not met or heard about. Their passion for mobilizing the people of God makes them good at what they do. For any missions pastor who wants to do a better job, there is a new organization called National Association of Missions Pastors (NAMP). For any missions pastor who seeks the fellowship and creative input of people of the same vision, I highly recommend NAMP. They have annual conferences, newsletters, and seminars. Their "big idea" is to help one another grow personally and professionally. Any church member can be a part of the association if their assignment includes responsibility for global missions. Here are some of the benefits of belonging to NAMP: resource material, regional and national forums, guidelines and mentoring to help you solve problems and build relationships with other missions pastors, and opportunities to assist other churches that may be experiencing something you have been through. If you are interested, contact NAMP, P.O. Box 3929, Peachtree City, GA 30269 (e-mail: NAMP@ACMC.org).

11

━━ THE DUGOUT ━━

MORE GREAT CHURCHES THAT COMPLETE THE TEAM

There's always a little controversy in the middle of the base-ball season when the All-Star Team is picked and the inter-league game is played. Outraged fans in bars, sports clubs, and living rooms across the nation are more than happy to give their opinion on what mistakes were made in the selec-tion of players. Making a call on great missions churches is not a lot different. I'm not kidding myself. I know that everyone will not agree with all my choices.

Just so that we can understand where I'm coming from, I'd like to review from *Missions in the 21st Century,* my ear-lier book, the nine criteria for a top-notch missions program.

Obviously not every church will do all nine things well, but here's the list:

1. The church must have an outward focus and strategy.
2. At least 30 percent of the church's budget must go to missions.
3. The church must have an ongoing training program for missionary candidates.
4. Missions education must be integrated into all the programs of the church.
5. The church must send its own people.
6. The church must be concerned about and pray for the lost.
7. The church must have a pastor who leads them in vision and outreach.
8. The church must be interested in helping other churches in missions.
9. The church must have a strong evangelism program in its community.

Now, on to the dugout:

Grace Chapel
3 Militia Drive
Lexington, MA 02421
Senior Pastor: Bryan Wilkerson
Director of Missions: Dr. David Jebaratnam

Grace Chapel is a two-thousand-member church just outside of Boston. The legacy of Paul Borthwick, the first full-time missions pastor at Grace, lives on under the leadership of David Jebaratnam. Borthwick was committed to educating the church about missions. He has written numerous books on missions, including *A Mind for Missions, How to Be a World Class Christian,* and *Six Dangerous Questions.* He was convinced that a church educated in missions would be mobilized.

Grace Chapel is a pacesetting church in the area of missions education for children. Missions is proactively integrated into all the children's programs and ministries. Grace Chapel, being a regional church in New England, is generous in sharing missions education opportunities with churches in the area. ACMC conferences and Perspectives courses are regularly held at Grace.

Grace Chapel sends out well-educated and trained short-term missions teams and keeps the people at home informed. One of David Jebaratnam's initiatives at Grace is to have every member mobilized for missions. The strategy has two thrusts: regional planning teams that seek to research and partner with ministries in the seven global regions of the world and the mobilization teams that seek ways to mobilize every member.

The most active group in this mobilization strategy is the sending teams. These teams are carefully trained to know about and care for missionaries on the field. These teams commit themselves to continuing education and training as well as active participation in the missionary's life. Neal Pirolo's book *Serving as Senders* is required reading for the sending teams and is part of the curriculum for training members of the sending teams.

My final call on Grace Chapel is that it is the place to be if you want a complete missions education from the cradle on up. Every program at Grace is soaked in missions education—you can't escape it.

Lake Avenue Church
393 North Lake Avenue
Pasadena, CA 91101
Senior Pastor: Gordon Kirk
Associate Pastor of Missions: Roger Bosch

John Piper, pastor of Bethlehem Baptist Church in Minneapolis, talks about living close enough to the Metrodome to hear the cheers and screams of the fans when the Minnesota Twins are winning.

Lake Avenue really doesn't have a chance not to be missions mobilized. They are within shouting distance of the U.S. Center for World Mission and Ralph Winter, its founder, attends Lake Avenue. They are also downwind from the Fuller Seminary School of World Missions. These two institutions have changed the course of world evangelization.

Lake Avenue has a rich heritage in missions. In 1903 they sent their first missionary to China. Lake Avenue was part of the founding of ACMC and hosted some of the first Perspectives on World Missions courses. It is also a mandate of the church that the senior pastor be a missions mobilizer—it is part of Lake Avenue's culture.

Because of the abundance of resources and personnel, their impressive list of hundreds of missionaries, and their large missions budget, it seems that there is not much more to say than that they do just about everything well. But recently, two initiatives have begun that demonstrate that when it comes to missions, Lake Avenue keeps on thinking.

In June of 1998 Senior Pastor Gordon Kirk announced to the congregation a dream he had that he called "Go 2003." The dream was that by 2003 every man, woman, and child at Lake Avenue would have been mobilized to have a cross-cultural experience. Roger Bosch, the missions pastor, says that from that day "everything changed" at Lake Avenue. At any one time a significant number of the congregation is overseas doing ministry, helping missionaries, doing medical work and professional services. The church has been mobilized and "being cross-cultural" is assumed. This is not an unorganized initiative. What has developed is what Roger calls "long-term–short-term missions." I believe it is an excellent model.

Lake Avenue's missions committee made strategic decisions to invest in certain ministries overseas for the long term. They have career missionaries working in those areas and have invested time and money in projects and outreach. So when people from the church want to do short-term or volunteer ministry overseas, they are plugged in to these long-term ministries. Even if members go for short-term trips, they are part of a long-term ministry.

I like that model. It is a good response to those who are critical of short-term missions as a shotgun effect that's all over the place and doesn't have focus. Lake Avenue has targeted their global ministries, and short-term missions become the reinforcements.

Finally, Lake Avenue has not missed their unique position and proximity to Hollywood and the entertainment business. They support a full-time "missionary to the stars" and an organization called Entertainment Ministries. Now, that's what I call getting into the game!

Christian Fellowship Church
4100 Millersburg Road
Evansville, IN 47725–7367
Senior Pastor: David Niednagel
Missions Pastor: Dave Mays

Christian Fellowship Church (CFC) is twenty-six years old, has more than three thousand in attendance, and has a missions budget of three-quarters of a million dollars. That was not always the story at CFC. Back in 1974, when they began with a few hundred people, they knew something should be done in missions but had no plan.

The rest of the story is a familiar one. Here are some comments from the missions chairman: "In the spring of 1979 someone brought me a brown three-ring notebook and said that ACMC, the organization that produced the notebook was having a conference; would I go as a delegate from the church?

"My wife and I went and we were overwhelmed. We had no idea that so many people in America were interested in missions. We went home with armloads of contacts and materials."

They followed the guidelines for developing a missions policy and leadership teams. Missions in the church flourished and most of the members of the original missions committee have gone overseas as missionaries! They began supporting a Jordanian student at Dallas Seminary who went back to start an evangelical seminary in Jordan. More from the church felt called into missions and were supported by the church.

The pastor, David Niednagel, began to take missionary trips to visit their missionaries all over the world and continues to participate in ACMC conferences. He recently said, "ACMC expanded our vision. Basically everything we have done in missions has been shaped by the instruction and help from ACMC. It is just invaluable. Without the conferences of ACMC, we wouldn't have had anywhere near the involvement and vision we have. I try to tell people every chance I get that ACMC is an organization whose purpose is to give themselves away in service to God's purpose on earth."

I'm happy to include this very enthusiastic endorsement of ACMC because I agree that missions without ACMC would be like baseball without a commissioner: It helps us all stay focused.

Calvary Church, Lancaster
1401 Esbenshade Road
Lancaster, PA 17601
Senior Pastor: John Miller
Missions Pastor: David M. Hall

There is no easy way to explain Calvary Church, Lancaster. It is nearing its seventieth year and has sent out many of those we call "heroes" in missions: Chet Bitterman, Jim Reapsome, Eileen Coon, Linell and Martha Davis, and so many more. Their missions budget is well over a million dollars and is at least 50 percent of the total church giving. But, as Dave Hall explains, "We're not sophisticated; we really don't have a budget." Our financial policy is "as the Lord enables."

It could be said that Calvary Church grew out of a missions conference. Men and women who had come together for a Bible and missions conference decided to form a church when they saw the need to add some continuity to the missions vision that was emerging from the conference. The first pastor, Dr. Robert Torrey, said, "Missions is a matter of life and death for the local church."

The annual eight-day conferences are not only to build and encourage the church's missions program but to refresh missionaries through Bible teaching and missions education. Annually around three hundred missionaries come to the church, are housed and fed by the church members for the eight-days, and are taught and ministered to from the Word. Missionaries are the honored guests. The missions conference is really a Bible conference for missionaries.

Calvary Church has one missionary fund and out of that fund the missionaries receive what they need. Young people going out from the church today are told, "Go out and raise what you can and then we'll see what we can do about the rest."

In the first fifty years of its life, 15.5 million dollars were given to missions.

Recently Jim Reapsome wrote to me about his introduction to Calvary Church when he was a college student. I think he explains Calvary best:

> My own understanding of world missions grew from my interaction with the missionaries that Calvary Church invited to the church for its week-long Bible and missionary conference. One church member in particular, a single woman with a heart for missions, kept the missionary flame burning by hosting students and missionaries in her home for the week-long gatherings. She provided the setting and God worked powerfully in this low-key context. Many of the students subsequently became missionaries. She also correlated monthly prayer letters and sent them around to all the students who had become missionaries.
>
> Another major influence I received from Calvary Church was the central focus given to missionary prayer in the Sunday morning worship service and the Wednesday night prayer meetings. The first fifteen minutes of the Sunday morning service were given to specific prayers for the church's many missionaries. On Wednesday night people spread across the sanctuary in couples and prayed for their missionaries. Many of these people could pray for the whole list from memory. The lasting influence I received from Calvary Church was that world missions was the heart of the church's reason for existence and that people cared enough for their missionaries to be informed about their needs and pray for them by name.

I guess missions at Calvary Church is like family. Everybody knows your name, you have significance and importance, and when it comes to finances, they always find a way to meet your needs. Maybe they're not the most sophisticated in their approach to missions, but they provide something more important for a missionary—everybody knows your name.

Wooddale Church
6330 Shady Oak Road
Eden Prarie, MN 55344
Senior Pastor: Dr. Leith Anderson
Missions Pastor: Tom Correll

Leadership development is part of the ethos of Wooddale Church. Their focus in international missions is in "training and equipping leaders of emerging churches to minister within their own community." As their strategy statement says, "Wooddale missions is about working together in a multitude of creative partnerships to build relationships that change lives forever. It's using our gifts and abilities—doing what we do best."

Senior Pastor Leith Anderson is passionate about empowering his own people and the people they touch globally to seek excellence in their service and ministry. By 2002 Wooddale hopes that it will have met its goal to plant twenty-four hundred new churches and train four hundred pastors in Romania. This is part of an international outreach that includes supporting a postgraduate training center in East Asia, partnering with a sister church in Guatemala, assisting struggling believers in Bulgaria and Vietnam, and reaching out to the more than 250,000 Sikhs in greater Vancouver. Wooddale is in the middle of another expansion project on their twenty-six-acre site, but in spite of that have pledged approximately 1.2 million dollars to world missions.

One initiative that Wooddale has pioneered is the Minnesota Coalition for Eastern Europe. Churches, foundations, individuals, and organizations have become a part of this effort to train leaders and plant churches in Eastern Europe.

A benefit that Wooddale has is that Leith Anderson is a cultural specialist. He understands the culture of the American church and is aware that excellence in leadership and quality in ministry will motivate the next generation of missionaries and their supporters. He works hard to keep a profile of high standards for missions in the church. Tom Correll, the missions pastor, is a team player, and together, they get the job done.

The Elmbrook Church
777 South Barker Road
Brookfield, WI 53045
Senior Pastor: Dr. Stuart Briscoe
Associate Pastor of Missions Ministries: Val Hayworth

Although Elmbrook Church does a lot of things very well, the thing that jump-started their missions initiative back in 1971 was the introduction of faith promise giving. Since that time, giving has grown dramatically and today Elmbrook gives around 1.6 million dollars a year to missions.

Elmbrook is a forty-year-old church with about six thousand members. In 1980 they became serious about developing a strategy for missions. They invited Dr. Robertson McQuilkin from Columbia International University to lead them in setting objectives and goals and developing a missions policy.

One of the results of that planning is support teams. Each member-missionary from Elmbrook has a group of twenty-five to thirty people behind him or her that keeps in close communication, makes sure the missionary's needs are before the congregation, and encourages the missionary. One missionary in Papua New Guinea was Medivaced to Australia for surgery because the support team heard about the need and got on the case.

Val Hayworth describes the direction Elmbrook wants to take with support teams: "Picture in your mind one hundred missionaries who are members of Elmbrook Church. Each missionary has an average of twenty-five members on his or her support team. Some members on the team have benefited from the missionary's ministry when they were on home assignment; some were discipled by the missionary. Some may be family members. This team encouraged the missionary as they prepared to go overseas. They committed resources to support the missionary on the field. The team plans for housing when the missionary comes home and possibly helps find a car. They send occasional books and tapes and maybe dig into their pockets for a medical emergency."

This is what is happening at Elmbrook and is an excellent model for any size church. Teams could be smaller and the job description different, but it has worked effectively.

Overlake Christian Church

9900 Willows Road NE
Redmond, WA 98052
Senior Pastor: Rick Kingham
Pastor of Strategic Partnerships: Dr. Tom Adelsman

Notice that Tom Adelsman's title is not missions pastor but pastor of strategic partnerships. That's your first clue to one of the two main thrusts of global outreach at Overlake. I could sum up Overlake with two words: *partnerships* and *professionals*.

Overlake is about thirty years old and has more than six thousand in attendance. Tom says his personal vision in his ministry is "to help Overlake and other churches fulfill their biblical vision through strategic partnerships." What this means is networking, and that is Tom's gift. His desire is to find Christian organizations, parachurch organizations, and Christian professionals and match them up with churches and missionaries with the same goals.

An example: Jim Roths, a businessman at Overlake, was willing to go to Uzbekistan, a country that Overlake had identified as a focus for their outreach, and set up businesses and an NGO (nongovernmental organization). He became the man on the ground for other businessmen who were willing to get involved with what he had started. He now has a large NGO that has been registered by the government.

Another example: Dr. Harlan Gephardt has developed a medical outreach ministry that goes overseas three times a year with a team of doctors to do clinics.

Because Overlake has been blessed with a significant population of professionals, missions takes on a professional outlook. The challenge was to network Overlake professionals with needs that their experiences and training could meet. This is Tom's cup of tea and giftedness.

I have seen a number of new ministries coming along with the purpose of sending business and medical professionals overseas. Luis Palau's AD 2000 had a business and medical arm. I believe this is a trend for the future. The profile of what a missionary is and does may be changing, and Overlake is an example of a church that has not let that possibility slip by. It would be good for churches to keep an eye on what happens at Overlake in strategic partnerships in the next few years.

Rolling Hills Covenant Church

2222 Palos Verdes Drive North
Rolling Hills Estates, CA 90274
Senior Pastor: Byron MacDonald
Pastor of International Outreach: Joe Handley

To help you understand the excitement about missions at Rolling Hills, let me excerpt from a letter written by Joe Handley, the missions pastor, to the church. After an evaluation of what he feels is a "crisis in missions thinking" due to millennium fever (a belief that time is running out), he talks about the privilege Rolling Hills has to be located in greater Los Angeles. It's the kind of letter that could only come out of Southern California. Here is his comment from, "Why I'm so jazzed about being at Rolling Hills Covenant Church."

> The cool thing is that in the middle of this crisis of mission thinking . . . the Lord is bringing the nations to us. Several of the unreached peoples of the world now live in our own backyard. Greater L.A. provides an unparalleled opportunity to begin reaching these normally inaccessible nations. Los Angeles is the most ethnically diverse city in human history, hosting people from some 140 countries, speaking more than 135 languages. It is home to more than 23 distinct Asian cultures alone. Amazingly it is the second largest Mexican, Armenian, Guatemalan, Cambodian, Korean, Filipino, and Salvadorian city in the world.
>
> Even in my neighborhood alone, I have conducted some informal ethnographic surveys while praying for our block. These surveys confirm this information about L.A. We have Norwegian, Polish, Irish, Japanese, British, Colombian, Mexican, Filipino, Native American, Indian (Hindu), Hasidic Jews, and Egyptian people living in our neighborhood.
>
> Recently I met with Timothy Ith, a church planter in Cambodia whom we support through Partners Interna-

tional. Timothy was a Buddhist who escaped Cambodia during Pol Pot's reign of terror and became a Christian in Atlanta. Today the Lord has blessed Cambodia because Timothy received the gospel here in the USA. Five churches have been planted and nine more are being developed under his leadership. He also serves as the president of Phnom Penh Bible College, the only Bible College in Cambodia.

. . . It is important that we have both a global and local missions advance. We stand at a unique time and place that has incredible global influence. We can make a difference if we continue our missions engagement both locally and globally being led by the Spirit.

I don't know about you, but I get excited about missions just reading that. One of my nine characteristics of a missions-minded church is that they are locally as well as globally minded. One focus charges and excites the other. Rolling Hills Covenant Church's dream to "light the Bay" with the gospel and to reach Kazakhstan (their adopted people group) keep the people "jazzed," as Joe would say. As far as I'm concerned, Rolling Hills is "exhibit A" for local/global thinking. Joe says, "We're a catalytic missions church. We live and breathe missions. Missions is what we are."

Asbury United Methodist Church
5538 S. Sheridan Road
Tulsa, OK 74145
Senior Pastor: Thomas Harrison
Director of Global Outreach: Mary Ann Smith

"Put your back up against the wall because I'm going to shoot you now!" Mary Ann Smith is telling the story of getting Bruce Olson's picture taken (about whom the book *Bruchko* was written). Bruce was on home assignment and they needed an updated missionary photo for the church. Mary Ann had taken Bruce over to the photographer. Those words echoed in Bruce's mind, the very words he had heard in threats from his enemies in South America. She laughed when she remembered how wide Bruce's eyes got.

There are two things I would highlight about Asbury. First, Mary Ann Smith cares for each one of the missionaries that Asbury supports. Although Asbury is a large denominational church (six thousand or more members), one of the outstanding gifts Mary Ann has brought to the church is the personal care and attention that missionaries receive. Her office is filled with their pictures and her desk with their letters.

Second is Asbury's partnership with ministry in Estonia. The relationship began with support of Estonian seminary student Andrus Norak, who came to the United States to study. Norak went back to be a pastor in Estonia. He is now the president of the Baltic Methodist Theological Seminary. Asbury's support helped make that possible. The school now has seventy-two students. In 1994 Asbury's senior pastor, Thomas Harrison, went to visit the seminary to see what God was doing. That visit came after the bishop of the Methodist Church in Estonia came to Asbury just to thank them for all the church had done: scholarships for students, partnering to build a church, helping with buildings for the seminary, and sending people to help. Almost two hundred people from Asbury have gone on short-term missions to Estonia.

But the clincher came when Asbury's senior pastor went with his thirteen-year-old son to visit the believers there. It was on that visit that the pastor's son committed his life to Christ. As Mary Ann says, "That has put Estonia forever on our hearts. Our pastor is a board member of the Methodist seminary in Estonia."

That is only one of the many stories that Mary Ann can tell—how one by one, heart by heart, Asbury has become a missions-mobilized church.

Calvary Church of Souderton
820 Route 113
Souderton, PA 18964
Senior Pastor: Meredith Wheeler
Pastor of Outreach and Spiritual Formation: Matt Reed

I think Calvary Church of Souderton wrote the book on how to lead a church through change in the area of missions. In 1988 Pastor Meredith Wheeler came to a five-hundred-member, conservative, traditional church. Missions was set in stone. Pastor Wheeler brought around him leaders like Jay Desco, who teaches organizational leadership on the graduate level, and Matt Reed, the outreach pastor, with gifts in helping people through change. They prayed, planned, and dreamed. Slowly the paradigms began to shift. Missions is not a program of the church, it is the culture of the church; missions is not doing tasks, it's developing people. Meredith admits, "It was sometimes a messy process to get where we are. Change can be painful." Today Calvary Church has more than two thousand members, and the first Sunday of every month the entire offering goes to international missions.

Under Matt Reed's guidance, the International Missions Board at Calvary is divided into three teams: Communications and Education Team, Organizational Support Team, and Strategic Planning Team. A commitment to excellence in all these areas is moving Calvary Church into the twenty-first century with a model of missions leadership that I think many missions committees will want to emulate.

12

SPECIALISTS
Doing One Thing Well

The churches in this chapter have found their particular skill in missions and are throwing their strength into doing that one thing well. We all can't do everything. Some churches don't have the manpower, staff, or financial resources to do what others can do. Thinking, however, that if they can't do it all, they won't do anything is not a good mind-set for churches. Sometimes churches are ethnically or culturally landlocked and can't reach out cross-culturally in their neighborhoods. Some churches are filled with new believers who still need months of missions education, and others have many young families or many senior citizens. A good manager, like Earl Weaver, looks at the people he has on the team and finds where the strengths are and uses them to the team's advantage. So look at your team, plan a strategy that works for you, and like these churches, play ball!

Pascack Bible Church
181 Piermont Avenue
Hillsdale, NJ 07642
Senior Pastor: Dr. Fred Beveridge

Pascack Bible Church, a church of about 350 members, is 33 years old. Fifty percent of its budget goes to missions. A decision was made a few years ago to make ministry to Albania the major focus of the church. It also began a process of total involvement on the part of the people. Pastor Fred Beveridge says that people in his church want to be part of what they are supporting. An exciting story of how God brought Albania into the life of the church has been printed, talked about, shown through slides and video, and is what has made missions come alive at Pascack.

They have begun to network with Gateway Cathedral on Staten Island, New York, where the largest Albanian community in the United States exists. The plan is to establish a ministry with full-time Albanian workers. Pascack Bible Church, which was committed to missions from its beginnings, has now moved into a new level of involvement and giving. Even a small church can do one thing well. Pascack is proof of that.

Church of the Savior
651 North Wayne Avenue
Wayne, PA 19087
Senior Pastor: Rich Craven
Missions Pastor: Robert Tickner

"It's futile to mobilize for missions if you don't have a heart for the lost." Missions Pastor Robert Tickner's biggest concerns are heart issues. Church of the Savior has a model missions program. They have adopted the Sudanese people and recruited and sent their own people to Indonesia, sending them in teams if at all possible. They focus on missions education and have a wonderful week-long missions conference and regular Perspectives courses. Their missions budget is almost one million dollars.

Robert Tickner is not quite satisfied. He believes there must be more spiritual development as part of a missions candidate's training. "If we spent less time recruiting and more time training, there would be less failure on the field. There is a high cost in not sending the right people," he adds.

One of the most creative ideas that Church of the Savior has is that the people who put on the missions conference are not the missions committee people. They are people from other departments of the church, people in arts and worship for example. This keeps missions from being owned by a certain few and enables missions to be identified with the whole body. I think that is one of the most effective ways to keep missions a part of the whole church.

Family Bible Church
240 Reed Street
Willow Grove, PA 19090
Senior Pastor: Greg Austin

Family Bible Church began with a clear "missions not mortgage" philosophy. Before they had even finished their first year, they had sent out their first missionary. Rich Sybesma, one of the founding members, admits that there was maybe more heart than head in the decision, but the passion of the new, young church was "to grow and send missionaries."

God honored their desire not to spend money on a church building and literally gave them a church. They paid one dollar to make the transaction legal. More than 30 percent of their budget goes to missions, and they regularly send out their own as well as support missionaries through missions agencies. At Family Bible Church they are all about missions.

Greg Austin, the present pastor, cautions that missions, their greatest strength and overriding priority, could also be a weakness. He asks, "Can you be too missions minded?" His concern is legitimate. Missions should not be done at the expense of the church's own neighborhood or even the needs in the body. Austin's organizational and management gifts are bringing structure to this little church with a huge heart.

Black Rock Congregational Church
3685 Black Rock Turnpike
Fairfield, CT 06432
Senior Pastor: Dr. Stephen A. Treash
Pastor of Global Missions: Larry Fullerton

Black Rock Congregational Church is known far and wide for its exciting and creative week-long missions conference. Every department and ministry in the church becomes involved in planning and putting on the conference. It is attended by churches within a regional consortium of churches. Black Rock has mobilized the consortium so that missionaries on furlough can concentrate their efforts in one region rather than travel all over the country. It is a model to be followed.

The missions conference at Black Rock tells me that people put their hearts into what they love, what they are passionate about. You can't attend the annual missions conference at Black Rock and come away without knowing that the people at Black Rock are sold out to world evangelization.

The Tabernacle Church
107 Seekel Street
Norfolk, VA 23505
Senior Pastor: Rich Hardison
Missions Pastor: Mike Latsko

What would you think if you met a medical doctor who had seven kids and every one of them was a doctor? Or a pastor and all of his sons became pastors? I'd be thinking that those fathers must have made their jobs seem like the greatest jobs on earth. Those kids would have seen their dad in the ups and downs of life and still chose to follow in his footsteps.

Well, the Tabernacle Church of Norfolk, or the Tab as its seven daughter churches affectionately call it, modeled missions in such a way that every one of the church plants considers missions one of its top priorities—and felt that way from day one. The church was founded by Rev. John Dunlap, who had wanted to be a missionary but was not able to go. So he stayed home and "grew missionaries."

Mike Latsko, the present missions pastor at The Tabernacle Church, admits that all of their missions programs are probably not as "state of the art" as some, and some strategies might be old-fashioned, but missions is in the blood of the church. Children, young people, and all the adult ministries of the church are steeped in the stories and the history of missions at the Tab. Someone said to me, "If you grow up at the Tab, missions is your arms and legs."

That is a legacy that any dad would praise God to be able to leave behind.

New Hope Church
16787 Bernardo Drive
Suite 14
San Diego, CA 92128
Senior Pastor: Joe Rhodes

New Hope has built their whole ministry around short-term missions. Joe Rhodes, the pastor, tells how he came to New Hope and found the people excited about missions, but he just didn't get it. Out of a sense of obligation, probably to appease the congregation, he went, reluctantly, to Lithuania in 1994.

And, as he says, "God tore my heart open. As I listened to these pastors—some who had been Christians for only two years—I felt like I was hearing the gospel for the very first time! I came home ready to mobilize the congregation."

That year he preached a series of thirteen messages on missions, and things have never really been the same since. The church was already excited about missions; now the pastor was on board.

Since that time, the church has networked with Global Missions Fellowship (GMF) and has made short-term missions their focus. Almost every month a new team is sent out to do ministry under the guidance of GMF. The children's pastor went to Lithuania, retired from the church, and moved there! With every team that goes out, there is a twenty-four-hour prayer chain back home to support them.

What I like about New Hope is that they are convinced about what their particular calling is. They networked with GMF, an excellent agency that could help them fulfill their calling through training and contacts, and then the congregation jumped in 100 percent. There's an energy here that is palpable.

South Hills Community Church
6601 Camden Avenue
San Jose, CA 95120-1998
Senior Pastor: Dr. Justin Dennison
Pastor of International Ministry: Mark Weimer

South Hills Community Church has developed an excellent missions policy and strategy statement. In fact it is one of the sample policies that ACMC uses as a model for churches to use when beginning to develop their own policy. Mark Weimer, the present missions pastor, is the former president of a Fortune 500 company—so there's no doubt that this church is striving for quality in missions ministry. Mark constantly keeps before the people the belief that they are called to do something greater than themselves, to "give yourself away for the advancement of the kingdom." This is a young vibrant church, set in the Silicon Valley, where the sky is the limit. Computer programmers and experts in design make sure that missions displays and publications are top quality.

Mark tells the story of one of the digital animation designers for the movie *Antz,* who took a year off to go to France and participate in a ministry outreach, through music, opera, and culture. It was an arts-and-media outreach based in the 120-acre Chateau de Granes in France. This certainly is not your ordinary missions outreach, yet people are coming to know Christ as teams of musicians and artists go from South Hills to participate in this unique ministry.

South Hills has a large investment in an unreached people group in the Philippines. The Agta tribe, hidden in the mountains, were unreached by modern culture and language. An IBM software designer from South Hills was encouraged to do a short-term mission to the Philippines with Wycliffe. While there, helping translators use computers, he and his wife "discovered" this tribe and felt called of God to do something. The tribe is fourteen miles by boat from anywhere and are like "the tribe that time forgot." Yet today Mark Weimer says you can't spend much time at South Hills before you know about the Agta tribe. The church has sent teams; bought rice fields for the people; built a school, shelters, and a clinic; and are supporting a Filipino pastor. They have made videos and done presentations to share the vision with the people.

Mark's dream is to take the many individual building blocks of the missions ministry at South Hills and tie them together in a single strategy. They are doing many creative things all over the world, but they want more focus. An overriding goal is to see thirty churches planted in the next year.

A church that has Luis Palau as one of the missionaries they support can't miss the big picture. The challenge, when there is so much creativity and talent in the church, is to find the single focus that ties it all together. Mark Weimer can do just that. Keep your eye on South Hills Community Church; there are exciting days ahead.

Cherry Hills Community Church
3900 E. Grace Boulevard
Highlands Ranch, CO 80126
Senior Pastor: Jim Dixon
Missions Pastor: Gene Kissinger

Gene Kissinger realizes the big responsibility he has as the missions pastor of a church that is held in high regard as a missions-mobilized church. He says that, although the leadership has always waved the missions flag, the turning point came when ACMC was invited to come and "get us organized." Ray Howard, who was the regional ACMC representative "spent an enormous amount of time and effort with us. The process gave us purpose."

The second turning point was when Cherry Hills hosted a Perspectives course. Those two events gave direction and education, and things began to move at Cherry Hills.

Gene's gift is training. The church is his missions team and they understand the game plan. Gene explains that the church is full of boomers and busters with lots of kids, and "most of us are mortgaged to the hilt, and none of us have any time! We have lots of new Christians, many from Catholic backgrounds, so there is a big learning curve in teaching about missions."

In some ways, being free of traditions and expectations has been a benefit. Missions education takes place from the ground up and the people take it seriously. Gene has the missions department organized into teams—twenty of them—covering every area of missions ministry at the church.

Nancy Fritz is the resident "missions maniac" in charge of children's missions. Nancy went to the International Children's Expo (see chapter 4) and came back on fire. Gene is very proud of the children's program at Cherry Hills.

"Time is our number one challenge in missions. We have to find a place for missions between soccer practice, ballet, piano lessons, second jobs, and commuting time. We're always in a battle for time," says Gene.

Cherry Hills is doing an excellent job with the people group they have adopted. They are called the Chantik (a pseudonym for an unreached Muslim group in Southeast Asia). Gene has spearheaded a consortium of churches who are all working on reaching the Chantik. When you walk into Cherry Hills Church, the Chantik are immediately visible through displays and information materials.

Under the excellent management and leadership style of Gene Kissinger, Cherry Hills is doing an amazing job in missions mobilization. Gene is aware of the unique challenges facing a busy, young church with many new believers. But the exciting stories of lives changed through short-term missions are a testimony to what God can do when a church is willing to make missions a priority at all costs.

Northwest Bible Church
8505 Douglas
Dallas, TX 75226
Senior Pastor: Neil Tomba
Minister of Missions: David R. Fletcher

This two-thousand-member, mostly college educated, church has a strategic plan that focuses on training national leaders, training North Americans to do ministry with nationals, and doing administrative support. They take particular interest in supporting theological education in Third World countries. The Asian Christian Academy, a seminary-level training school is a place where they have put a lot of resources.

The most interesting fact about Northwest Bible Church is their definite choice *not* to be involved in the 10/40 window (that part of the world from West Africa to east Asia—from 10 to 40 degrees latitude north—in which 97 percent of the world's unreached and unevangelized people live. For more information, go to www.ad2000.org/1040ovr.htn). The missions leadership feel that it will be Chinese and Indian believers who will break through that window, and our Western attempts do not show sufficient success for all the effort and resources that have been put into it. As Dave Fletcher says, "We'll pray! We do pray, but God has not led our church to involvement in the 10/40 window. I'm not convinced this is where we should be at this time. We can train leaders in India and China, but westerners may have to stand aside and let others see God work through them to break through 'the window.'" Northwest Bible Church has an excellent partnership with the Asian Christian Academy in Bagalur, India. It is a partnership with accountability to the West but not control from the West. It's an excellent model.

The Mosaic Church (Church on Brady)
715 Brady Avenue
East Los Angeles, CA 90022
Pastor: Erwin McManus

This Southern Baptist Church has sent out more of its own missionaries than any other church within the denomination—and it is certainly not the largest. This multiethnic church in inner-city East Los Angeles has been well taught by former pastors and missions executives like Tom Wolfe and Carol Davis. They do an excellent job in missions education and training by making use of the many ethnic communities in their neighborhood. Missionary candidates are put through a four-stage mentoring process. The stages are head (intellectual challenges), heart (integrity issues), hands (skills assessment), and home (relationship building). It is working so well that at any time about 15 percent of the congregation is on the mission field.

The Mosaic Church is a terrific example of a church that has used its unique local culture to develop world Christians.

Emmanuel Faith Community Church
639 E. Felicita
Escondido, CA 92025
Senior Pastor: Dennis Keating
Missions Pastor: Harry Larson

"Harry, now that we know what we know, we can never go back to missions as usual." Harry Larson, the missions pastor, describes that moment when a member of the missions committee came to him and made that statement in the middle of the ten-week Perspectives on World Missions course. Sixty-five people from the church were taking the course. Harry, who had been a missionary, was almost embarrassed to admit that all his preconceived ideas about missions were being exploded as well. His biblical, historical, and cultural paradigms were being challenged, but more than that, he was "blown away by the concept of strategy."

Harry laughs when he admits, "I was almost embarrassed that I was being paid to do what I was doing."

But then things began to change. Instead of the "how many pins do we have on the map?" strategy, the church began to pray and ask God for focus and direction. For weeks they met weekly for two and three hours and prayed. They studied the Adopt-a-People program, about missions education, and about being missions—not missionary—centric.

Harry talks about times in the past when the church would call up a mission agency and say, "Do you have any missionaries in France? We don't have anybody in France." And the mission agency would assign them a missionary to France, sight unseen. And there would be another pin on the map.

I don't think Emmanuel Faith, a five-thousand-member, sixty-year-old church, was alone back in those days.

What thrills me about Harry Larson and the team at Emmanuel is their great determination to learn, change, and pray. They were one of the first churches to develop a written contract between the agency, the church, and the missionary or missions team. It is an excellent tool for making sure all parties are moving with the same goals and understanding. Emmanuel Faith is one of the best missions churches in their area because they are not afraid to make changes and grow.

The Chapel (in Akron)
135 Fir Hill
Akron, OH 44304
Senior Pastor: Knute Larson
Associate Pastor of Missions: Bob Schneider

"Tom, I've reached my goal and at this point everyone in leadership at the Chapel has been overseas." I can remember Bob Schneider's joy to have met that goal in his ministry. He is convinced (and rightly so) that getting the leadership of the church, especially the senior pastor, overseas to experience missions firsthand is one of the most effective ways to mobilize a church for missions. Bob also seeks out leaders among laypeople in the church and finds a reason to send them overseas as well, for example a comptroller who was needed in Ethiopia and a music teacher in Eastern Europe. Bob believes what George Verwer, the founder of Operation Mobilization, has said: "You must send a member of the staff overseas every year. Keep sending them. The memory fades."

Bob is a cutting edge guy and his leadership at the Chapel affects many churches in the area. The Chapel is a regional church that reaches out to other churches in training, mobilizing, and encouragement. They have hosted Perspectives courses, ACMC conferences, and Adopt-a-People initiatives. Bob says that involvement with ACMC has been "the single most significant factor in the growth of the missions program."

The Chapel has an excellent internship program for potential missionaries. At any one time they may have seven to ten interns. Members need to be interns for one year before they are commissioned to go overseas.

Bob says that one of his greatest joys as a missions pastor at the Chapel is that the church is across the street from the University of Akron. Sometimes there are as many as eighty countries represented among the students there. That's every missions pastor's dream come true—eighty countries across the street!

The Chapel has recently sent teams to Macedonia and Albania. They consider church planting their first priority in missions. They have adopted six unreached people groups. You can't be around Bob long before you're excited about the potential when you get your people excited about missions.

Candia Congregational Church

P.O. Box 102
Candia, NH 03034
Senior Pastor: Rev. David Runnion-Barefoot
Missions Coordinator: Liz Claver

Candia is "the little church that could." When Liz Claver, the missions chairperson, came to me at an ACMC conference a number of years ago, she was discouraged. She said, "Our missions budget this year was one hundred dollars—and we didn't spend it all!" She said that missions was at the bottom of the priority list at Candia—right after the coffee hour. We talked about a strategy that included getting other churches in the area to cooperate to get speakers and materials for an area-wide conference. Liz was ready to move and she mobilized the churches for fifty miles around. Things began to happen. The last time I spoke with Liz, their missionary giving was over thirty thousand dollars—and they're a small New England church.

Pastor Runnion-Barefoot adds another story to explain the change at Candia. He calls it, "Finding the Missionary in Your Closet." He believes it can be a key to unlocking the hearts of old, established, and sometimes cold mainline churches. At some point in almost every church's history, there was a time when missions was paramount. Historically in America that has been the case. Pastor Runnion-Barefoot searched back in the archives of the Candia church—a church established in 1771—and found that in 1826 a daughter of one of the prominent families in the church went to serve overseas as a missionary. She was one of their own. Descendants of that family are members in the church today. That connection excited and cemented in many of the members' minds the fact that missions was an important part of who they were. Now, that's not going to do it in many corners of the country, but for New England, that pushed missions ahead like many other things never could.

Maybe the lesson here is that size and age should never be excuses for not figuring out what can make missions happen in your church.

Northside Community Church
5185 Peachtree Dunwoody Road NE
Atlanta, GA 30342
Pastor: John Rowell

You can't talk about missions and Northside without mentioning John Rowell's book *Magnify Your Vision for the Small Church* (1999). This is the story of a church that made a decision to fall in love with Bosnia—and that was before Bosnia was in the news. They have thrown their hearts into the ministry to that country. Their story will make you laugh, cry, and then say, "We could do something like that too." It's a reminder that small churches can do big things.

Briarwood Presbyterian Church
2200 Briarwood Way
Birmingham, AL 35243
Missions Pastor: Thomas Cheely

I'll end with the ultimate. Briarwood is not a church—it's a village, a missions experience. I give this church credit for never letting down on their missions giving, even when they have been in multimillion-dollar building programs. They have a three-million-dollar missions budget and they support 280 missionary units, of which 91 are members of the church. Through these missionaries, they are involved with 65 missions agencies.

Much of this extensive missions involvement came from the founding pastor Frank Barker. People say he ate, drank, slept, and even dreamed missions.

Today, Missions Pastor Tom Cheely has as his team a missions committee composed of seventy-five people involved with world missions, forty in national ministries, twenty-five in urban ministries, and seventeen with international students. Tom says these people are "his congregation." People at Briarwood are on a "waiting list" to be accepted onto the missions committee. As Tom says, "It's the thing we do."

Out of all the superlatives that could be used for Briarwood's missions ministry, one that excites me is their intentional interest in internationals that move to Birmingham. The church has made it their objective to see that every international student, immigrant, settler, international business person, or refugee that comes to Birmingham is welcomed by someone from the church, invited to the church, and offered hospitality. By an amazing story of God's grace, a wonderful feat of organization and planning, this has been happening.

Tom acknowledges the joy it is to work with the team he has in a church like Briarwood.

I praise God that even with all the blessings God has poured on Briarwood at home, they have never lost sight of the nations and God's great agenda that all the nations will glorify his Son.

COOPERSTOWN
What's Baseball without the Statisticians?

If you don't feel an aura that's almost spiritual when you walk through the Hall of Fame in Cooperstown, then check tomorrow's obituary; you're in it.

Don Sutton, Baseball Hall of Famer

Located in central New York State, Cooperstown has become a shrine to baseball lovers from all over the world. Baseball is statistics, records, compilations, and lists. Cooperstown has them all. You can't spend any time with a true baseball fanatic before you're "into it"—arguing about who hit what and when they hit it and where!

Bill James, Pete Palmer, and others have made it their life work to compile and analyze the statistics. It's part of true baseball.

Dave Mays is the Bill James of missions. He's a former chemical engineer who went to an ACMC conference, got blown away, retired from his career and plunged into missions with passion. He is presently the Great Lakes representative for ACMC.

Dave's gift is statistics, records, and analysis and he brings that to his role as a missions mobilizer. He keeps lists of missions books, ideas for conferences, good speakers, videos, organizations, resources, quotes from the Bible that challenge us to do missions, names of agencies, and you name it. He even has lists of lists. If there's anything you need to know about missions—Dave has it. Recently, at the urging of many of us who are organizationally challenged, Dave compiled many of his lists on a disc. It's a wealth of wonderful missions information and can be ordered from ACMC. Ask for *Stuff You Need to Know about Missions: A Handbook of Lists*. What follows are some excerpts from missions book lists on Dave's disc. It's a better selection than I could ever have given you. But then, I'm no Bill James.

All-time Great Books

Paul Borthwick. *Six Dangerous Questions.*
Michael Griffiths. *Get Your Church Involved in Missions.*
Patrick Johnstone. *The Church Is Bigger than You Think.*
Walter Kaiser. *Mission in the Old Testament.*
John Piper. *Let the Nations Be Glad.*
John Rowell. *Magnify Your Vision for the Small Church.*

Missions Books for Pastors

Johannes Blauw. *The Missionary Nature of the Church.*
Paul Borthwick. *How to Be a World Class Christian.*
David Bryant. *Stand in the Gap.*
William Owen Carver. *Missions in the Plan of the Ages.*
Richard DeRidder. *Discipling the Nations.*

Robert Hall Glover. *The Bible Basis of Missions.*

H. Cornell Goerner. *All Nations in God's Purpose.*

Ian Hay. *Isaiah and the Great Commission.*

Roger Hedlund. *The Mission of the Church in the World.*

Patrick Johnstone. *Operation World.*

David Mays. *Building Global Vision.*

Robertson McQuilkin Jr. *The Great Omission.*

John R. Mott. *The Pastor and Modern Missions.*

Andrew Murray. *The Key to the Missionary Problem.*

A. B. Simpson. *Missionary Messages.*

Bill and Amy Stearns. *Catch the Vision 2000.*

Tom Telford. *Missions in the 21st Century.*

Ruth Tucker. *From Jerusalem to Irian Jaya.*

Georg Vicedom. *The Mission of God.*

Tom Wells. *A Vision for the Nations.*

Theodore Williams. *The Local Church and Mission.*

Great Missions Books from the Last Five Years

2000

James Engel. *Changing the Mind of Missions.*

Scott Moreau, ed. *Evangelical Dictionary of World Missions.*

Neal Pirolo. *The ReEntry Team: Caring for Your Returning Missionaries.*

Daniel Rickett. *Building Strategic Relationships.*

1999

Luis Bush. *The Move of the Holy Spirit in the 10/40 Window.*

Bruce Camp. *Discover Our Place in His Plans.*

David Forward. *Essential Guide to Short Term Missions.*
Steve Hoke. *Send Me.*
David Mays. *How to Operate an Effective Missions Leadership Team.*
Scott Morton. *Funding Your Ministry.*
Robert Mundy. *All About Faith Promise Offerings.*
Jim Reapsome. *Final Analysis.*
John Rowell. *Magnify Your Vision for the Small Church.*
Tom Sine. *Mustard Seed vs. McWorld.*
Pete Sommer. *Getting Sent.*
Tom Steffen. *Business as Usual in the Missions Enterprise.*

1998

Scott Kirby. *Short Term Mission Adventure.*
Paul McKaughan. *Choosing a Future.*

1997

Lorry Lutz. *Women As Risk Takers for God.*
William Taylor, ed. *Too Valuable to Lose.*

1996

James Engel. *Clouded Future.*
Bryant Myers. *The New Context of World Missions.*
Jim and Carol Plueddemann. *Witnesses to All the World.*
Martha VanCise. *Successful Mission Teams.*

Missions Books People Love to Read

Gladys Alward. *Gladys Alward—The Little Woman.*
Neil Anderson. *In Search of the Source.*

Gladis DePree. *The Spring Wind.*
Ed and Doreen Dulka. *Colombian Jungle Escape.*
Steve Estes. *Called to Die.*
Thomas Hale. *Don't Let the Goats Eat the Loquat Trees.*
Thomas Hale. *Living Stones of the Himalayas.*
Thomas Hale. *On the Far Side of Liglig Mountain.*
Stephen Hugh. *Never Touch a Tiger.*
Bruce Olson. *Bruchko.*
Charles Partee. *Adventure in Africa.*
Don Richardson. *Peace Child.*
Mark Ritchie. *Spirits of the Rain Forest.*
Helen Roseveare. *Living Sacrifice.*
Ron Snell. *It's a Jungle Out There.*
Martin St. Kilda. *Under the Far Bamboo.*
Bill and Amy Stearns. *Catch the Vision 2000.*
David Thompson. *On Call.*
W. Terry Whalin. *One Bright Shining Path.*
J. Christy Wilson. *More to Be Desired than Gold.*

Missions Books to Stretch People

Don Richardson. *Eternity in Their Hearts.*
Bob Sjogren and Bill and Amy Stearns. *Run with the Vision.*

Most Influential Books on Missions

Theology and the Church

Johannes Blauw. *The Missionary Nature of the Church.*
William Carey. *An Enquiry into the Obligation of Christians to Use Means for the Conversion of the Heathens.*

W. O. Carver. *Missions in the Plan of the Ages.*
H. Cornell Goerner. *All Nations in God's Purpose.*
Andrew Murray. *Key to the Missionary Problem.*
George W. Peters. *A Biblical Theology of Missions.*
John Piper. *Let the Nations Be Glad.*

Missionary Stories

Elisabeth Elliot. *Through Gates of Splendor.*
Bruce Olson. *Bruchko.*
Don Richardson. *Peace Child* and *Eternity in Their Hearts.*
Martin St. Kilda. *Near the Far Bamboo.*

Missions History

J. Herbert Kane. *A Global View of Christian Missions.*
J. Herbert Kane. *The Progress of World-Wide Missions.*
Stephen Neill. *A History of Christian Missions.*
John Caldwell Thiessen. *A Survey of World Missions.*
Ruth Tucker. *From Jerusalem to Irian Jaya.*

Personal Growth and Involvement

David Barrett. *The World Christian Encyclopedia.*
Paul Borthwick. *A Mind for Missions.*
David Bryant. *Stand in the Gap.*
Amy Carmichael. *If.*
Michael Griffiths. *Get Your Church Involved in Missions.*
Patrick Johnstone. *The Church Is Bigger Than You Think.*
Patrick Johnstone. *Operation World.*
John R. Mott. *The Pastor and Modern Missions.*

John Stott. *Christian Mission in the Modern World.*
Stacy Warburton. *Making a Missionary Church.*

Great Books on Missionary Care

Marjorie F. Foyle. *Overcoming Missionary Stress.*

Peter Jordan. *ReEntry: Making the Transition from Missions to Life at Home.*

Kelly O'Donnell, ed. *Missionary Care: Counting the Cost for World Evangelization.*

Neal Pirolo. *The ReEntry Team: Caring for Your Returning Missionaries.*

Neal Pirolo. *Serving As Senders: Six Ways to Care for Your Missionaries.*

Esther Schubert. *What Missionaries Need to Know about Burnout and Depression.*

William D. Taylor. *Too Valuable to Lose: Exploring the Causes and Cures of Missionary Attrition.*

Tom Telford's father was a pastor and well-known evangelist, but Tom didn't become a Christian until later in his life. Then he felt constrained by the biblical mandate to take the gospel to the whole world. Self-educated in missions, Tom has invested his adult life in helping churches maximize their potential for world evangelization.

Beginning as missions chairman in his local church, Tom is now vice president of mobilization for United World Mission (UWM). Prior to his current position, he served fifteen years with ACMC (Advancing Churches in Missions Commitment) as Northeast Regional Director and Supervisor of Regional Ministries. With ACMC Tom inspired, challenged, and trained hundreds of churches to strengthen their commitment and approach to missions. Essentially that is what he continues to do through UWM.

A sought-after missions speaker and consultant for churches throughout the eastern United States, Tom has also lectured on world missions and the local church at Seminary of the East, Philadelphia College of the Bible, Westminster Seminary, and Columbia International University. He is a regular lecturer in the Perspectives on the World Christian Movement course.

Tom is married to Nancy and they have two grown children and three grandchildren.

Lois Shaw and her husband, Mark, have served with the Africa Inland Mission since 1980. They work at the Nairobi Evangelical Graduate School of Theology in Kenya, where Mark is a lecturer in church history and theology and Lois works in the development office. They have two grown children, Anne and Jonathan. Mark is still waiting for his beloved Red Sox to win the World Series!

United World Mission

establishing reproducing churches throughout the world

Tom Telford and United World Mission would like to help prepare and engage your church for global missions, working with your church to develop 3-way partnerships:

Your Local Church
+ UWM
+ An Unreached People
= Churches Planted Worldwide

Contact Tom Telford
UWM's Vice President of Church Mobilization
800-959-3523

or write us at:

United World Mission
PO Box 668767
Charlotte, NC 28266-8767
800-825-5896
www.uwm.org